*Experiencing the Blessings of the*
*Beatitudes of Jesus for Today*

# TED CREEN

GET A LIFE!
Copyright © 2013 by Ted Creen

All rights reserved. Neither this publication nor any part of this publication may be reproduced or transmitted in any form or by any means, electronic or mechanical, including photocopying, recording or any information storage and retrieval system, without permission in writing from the author.

Scripture taken from the HOLY BIBLE, NEW INTERNATIONAL VERSION®. Copyright © 1973, 1978, 1984 International Bible Society. Used by permission of Zondervan. All rights reserved.

Printed in Canada

ISBN: 978-1-77069-844-4

Word Alive Press
131 Cordite Road, Winnipeg, MB R3W 1S1
www.wordalivepress.ca

Cataloguing in Publication may be obtained through Library and Archives Canada

I dedicate this book to my wife and spiritual partner,
Lorraine, and to our growing community of faith at Huron
Feathers Presbyterian Centre, Sauble Beach, Ontario.
Together we will explore the Beatitudes of Jesus
and live out the promised blessings.

# TABLE OF CONTENTS

---

# FOREWORD

A NUMBER OF YEARS AGO, I REVISITED JESUS'S SERMON ON THE Mount as preserved for us in Matthew chapters five to seven. I decided that with some preparation I could memorize the entire sermon and deliver it during a church service. Armed with a few props and a bit of Biblical costuming, I took to the stage. It turned out to be a powerful experience. The depth of this teaching began to work in me. How simple and yet profound were those words of Jesus! Each time I have presented what I introduce as "the greatest sermon ever given," I hear from those present that many undergo the same kind of experience.

The Sermon on the Mount begins with the set of eight Beatitudes. Again, I am increasingly impressed with how powerful are those teachings. They are familiar to most of us, but that may be a danger—to leave them superficially familiar and not plumb into the deeper truths they contain. And so, over the past months, I set about digging into those Beatitudes. That has led to this book. It is my answer to those who make the request to "get a life." For unlike what is often inferred by that saying, the life offered in the Beatitudes is the fullest one possible.

I invite you to journey with me into these Beatitudes. I pray that you too will discover the deeper dimension of living offered to those who choose, as I will point out, to open the narrow gate and embark on an exciting yet potentially more difficult pathway that leads to receiving the blessings of Jesus.

This book will become the basis of a study group experience in my ministry, and I have prepared a study outline, which I can make available to anyone who contacts me.

May all of God's blessings be yours,

Ted Creen, tedcreen@hotmail.com

# PREFACE

---

*Now when Jesus saw the crowds, he went up on*
*a mountainside and sat down.*
*His disciples came to him, and he began to teach them saying:*
*Blessed are the poor in spirit, for theirs is the kingdom of heaven.*
*Blessed are those who mourn, for they will be comforted.*
*Blessed are the meek, for they will inherit the earth.*
*Blessed are those who hunger and thirst for righteousness,*
*for they will be filled.*
*Blessed are the merciful, for they will be shown mercy,*
*Blessed are the pure in heart, for they will see God.*
*Blessed are the peacemakers, for they will be*
*called the sons of God.*
*Blessed are those who are persecuted because of righteousness,*
*for theirs is the kingdom of God.*
*Blessed are you when people insult you, persecute you*
*and falsely say all kinds of evil*
*against you because of me. Rejoice and be glad,*
*because great is your reward in heaven, for in the same way they*
*persecuted the prophets who were before you.*
Matthew 5:1-11

# GATES AND PATHWAYS

1

*Enter through the narrow gate. For wide is the gate and broad
is the road that leads to destruction, and many enter through it.
But small is the gate and narrow the road
that leads to life, and only a few find it.*
Matthew 7:13-14

A FEW YEARS AGO, I STOOD AT A CHECKPOINT IN THE SOUTH
country of Peru. Passport and trekking permit in hand, I was
waiting to embark on a great adventure. I was about to hike
the Inca Trail to Machu Picchu! It was one of those once-in-
a-lifetime kind of ventures. Perhaps at the back of my mind
was the expression, "Get a life!" I admit that I have often felt
a need to step outside of the usual, to take new risks in order
to experience something deeper and more profound. There are
times to challenge the limits of your comfort zone. Perhaps
such desires have come to you as well. Maybe someone else has
attempted to prod you in that direction with, "Oh, why don't
you just get a life!"

I do admit to having some apprehensions about the Inca Trail. I had heard about the difficulties associated with high-altitude hiking. Stories abounded about trekkers getting into trouble up in the Andes Mountains. As I stood at that checkpoint there was a momentary twinge of, "What was I thinking?" However, there I was, ready to accomplish something I had been dreaming about for months.

Once through the checkpoint, you must cross a narrow suspension bridge spanning the Urubamba River, and then you are totally committed. However, I was with a friend from home, a good group of trekkers, a terrific guide, and a support group of porters and cooks. Yes, I did have to deal with altitude, particularly on the second day when we climbed over a high mountain pass. In the end though, the hike was all I had anticipated and more. We entered Machu Picchu as the sun rose on a glorious morning. It was so exhilarating that three years later I returned and hiked it again, this time with my daughter Sarah.

All of this came back to me as I began to meditate on a warning Jesus gives in his Sermon on the Mount (Matthew 7:13-14). He presents two pathways in life: one narrow and difficult, the other broad and easy. Two gates as well open up to those pathways, a wide one and a narrower one. The first impulse might be to choose the easier pathway through the wide gate. Human nature would often direct us away from risk and danger in order to seek security and comfort. Jesus cautions us about our choice, for the only pathway to life is through the narrow gate and up the rougher path. The wider path, though attractive, will ultimately lead to destruction. It is obvious that if we are to "get a life" we must first of all make a fundamental choice of direction. We must make a commitment.

## CHOICES: GENESIS 13:1-13

Every significant journey begins with a decision. The story of the people of God in the Old Testament originates with a call from God upon Abram (whom God renames Abraham). He is to gather together his family and possessions and begin a journey. It would be a journey of faith, seeing as God does not precisely tell Abraham where he will end up. After sojourns in Haran and Egypt, Abraham does arrive in the land God had promised. It was a journey of promise, for this call to Abraham included the vision that the generations following him would grow into a great nation.

Years of prospering followed. However, the time arrived when the families of Abraham and his nephew Lot had outgrown the ability of the land to support them. Disputes had arisen between them, and so the families would need to go their separate ways. Gazing over the expanse of land, Abraham suggested a division of territory: either the level plain along the Jordan River or the interior hill country. Going against the usual custom whereby Abraham, being the elder, would make the choice, he offered it to his nephew. It didn't take Lot long to decide. The plain was rich and fertile, a place of springs like a garden. Ideal pasture and easily available water did appear to be the correct choice for him to make. Let Abraham deal with the rougher hill country.

Life is based on the choices we make. Remember the alternatives of that broad, easy pathway that unfortunately leads to potential destruction? On that fertile plain so rich in pasture land lay the city of Sodom, renowned for its wickedness. We discover that Lot moved ever closer and eventually ended up inside the city. When God's judgement is pronounced on Sodom, Lot hesitated to leave, but Abraham pleaded before God for his safety. Even then an angel had to rush Lot out of the

GET A LIFE!

city before it would be destroyed. Unfortunately his wife turned back and ended up as a pillar of salt. Beware of the seemingly easy pathways of life. In another book, *Moving Mountains (or at least managing them)*, I labelled Lot's hasty choice of the easier pathway as one of those "it seemed like a good idea at the time" decisions that come back so often to bite us.

In *Pilgrim's Progress*, one of the classics of Christian literature, John Bunyan wrote the story of a peasant named Christian who set out on a journey to the Celestial City. At one point Christian faced a hill named Difficulty. As he and two other travellers approached that hill, he noticed that there were actually three paths leading up. A narrow pathway in the centre was steep and high, and the other travellers chose the easier side paths. Christian, however, took the narrow pathway and as he went, he said to himself: "The hill, though high, I covet to ascend. The difficulty will not me offend. For I perceive the way to life lives here: Come, pluck up, heart, let's neither faint nor fear. Better, though difficult, the right way to go. Than wrong, though easy, where the end is woe."[1]

**THE INVITATION**

Jesus issues an invitation for us to truly "get a life" through discovering the narrow, potentially difficult pathway. I want to focus on the initial verses of the Sermon on the Mount, the eight Beatitudes. They describe life on that narrow pathway. Each one indicates a way to unlock the blessings of God. The Beatitudes actually are exclamations proclaiming how God desires to give us blessings. The Greek text for the Beatitudes does not include the verb "are," so each of the beatitudes is a ringing, "Oh the blessedness of…"

The concept of blessing in the Bible is very important for us to understand. Receiving a blessing meant the conferring of

4

identity. A parent's blessing would give their child an essential sense of worth. God's blessing upon us identifies us as his children, called and chosen. A blessing confers purpose and destiny. To be blessed also indicates how cherished and loved we are by God, creating a deep bond of intimacy with him. In the Old Testament, God's blessing called into being his people, the nation of Israel. They were to carry the purpose of God to the world. God's blessing invited his people to maintain a constant and intimate relationship with him. They were chosen to continue that blessing generation to generation. Deuteronomy 28:1-14 lists blessings available to the people who continue to abide in God's purpose for them. There follows a set of warnings as well, curses that will occur if the people reject the blessing of God. As we shall see with the Beatitudes of Jesus, those blessings call us into being sons and daughters of God, citizens of his kingdom. The blessings come about through our living relationship with Jesus, as we will discover as we explore each Beatitude in turn.

The Greek word for blessing is *makarios*. Some have translated it as *happy*, but I do not feel that gives the true essence of the word. We tend to hook our feeling of happiness upon externals: wealth, possessions, circumstances, or status. We think that there must be something or someone to make us feel constantly happy. We gripe and complain if they fail to provide that. It will become apparent in our study of these Beatitudes that the blessing Jesus offers is something far deeper and more profound than simple happiness. We shall discover how this blessing, once received, is the gateway to living a full and abundant life.

It is surprising to discover just who it is in the Beatitudes that will receive the blessing. It will not necessarily be the rich, powerful, or successful people that our culture idolizes. Rather, it will be those who are poor, who are able to mourn, who live out meekness, or who endure persecution that will be blessed. It will be those who make the choice to journey inwardly to touch the deepest and most potentially painful places of life that Jesus offers his kingdom. Get a life? There is risk, danger, and struggle ahead on that pathway, but indeed, as Jesus said, it will lead us to life.

## WRESTLING THE BLESSING: GENESIS 32-33

Scripture illustrates the reality of risk and struggle. Another of the great Old Testament characters is Jacob, grandson of Abraham. His story has some very odd twists and turns. To begin with, God gave a blessing and a promise to Abraham that a great nation would arise through the generations of his family. That promise is to pass through Jacob, although he was not the oldest son of Isaac. Esau, his twin, was born just ahead of Jacob. However, aided and abetted by his mother Rebekah, Jacob tricked a blessing from his father that should have gone to Esau. When he discovered what had taken place and that the blessing was irrevocable, Esau was incensed and threatened to kill Jacob. Jacob fled to live with a relative named Laban.

Years passed as Jacob prospered in that place. His family became large, and his flocks multiplied. Finally, the time came for God to direct him to return home. However, that would pose a huge risk. The brother Jacob had cheated was still there. Had he let go of his bitterness? Obviously Esau had prospered as well, for news comes to Jacob that Esau is coming to meet him...with four hundred men! To prepare for meeting his brother, Jacob divided his family and flocks into two groups, hoping that one group would escape if Esau attacked. Then he prepared to spend a solitary night by the ford of the Jabbok River.

It was a very interesting night indeed for Jacob, as he spent those dark hours wrestling with a stranger. Seeing that he could not overcome Jacob, the stranger touched the socket of Jacob's hip, leaving him limping. At daybreak the stranger asked to be let go. Jacob, however, prevailed on this stranger, whom he now recognized as a messenger of God, if not God himself. Jacob requested a blessing, and it was granted. This time the blessing came not through deceit and trickery, but honestly through a hard-fought struggle.

Blessed be! Furthermore, the stranger conferred a new name upon Jacob. He would now be known as Israel, one who had struggled with God and overcome. Jacob now was fully ready to meet Esau (a peaceful meeting, thankfully) and to become the inheritor of God's blessing for the nation. As we explore the Beatitudes of Jesus, we will discover how God's blessings are offered for our lives today. We will also become aware that receiving those blessings will often come, like Jacob, through our wrestling with the deeper issues of living.

## SETTING OUT

I return to my reflections on the Inca Trail trek. Indeed, it was the invitation to take a risk, get a life, and to endure potential hardships that was a large part of the attraction. Should that not also be the case for our spiritual lives? Living the Beatitudes will involve investment and effort. Perhaps Thich Nhat Hanh is correct by stating that "the miracle isn't walking on water but walking on the earth, fully alive to every moment."[2]

Get a life! Decide now that you will move out from your old comfort zones into new dimensions of living. Accept the risk to embrace the full life Jesus offers. Choose to be one who will turn away from the broad path and choose to walk the narrow pathway with Jesus. Prepare to live the Beatitudes of blessing!

## CLENCHED FISTS OR OPEN HANDS?

2

*Blessed are the poor in spirit, for theirs is the kingdom of heaven.*
Matthew 5:3

GET A LIFE! THERE WAS A HUSH IN THE VAN AS WE PULLED AWAY from the city dump in Managua, Nicaragua. All of us were processing the experience we had just been through. In some ways I still am. I was with a mission group who had travelled to Nicaragua to help build school rooms for a small church. It was also an immersion in the realities of life in such a country. I was left with some deep reflections both upon my time in Nicaragua and following that, upon my life back home.

The dump is an incredible place. It is vast, with trucks rumbling in continually to add their loads. Smoke billows from fires set to reduce garbage to ash. Hundreds of black vultures circle overhead to join countless more on the ground feasting on the trash. As those trucks arrive, the residents of the dump—men, women, and children—pick through the refuse, seeking out anything that can be recycled for some income. We had brought large containers of water and offered them a cold drink.

What was I experiencing? Certainly there was a pang of emotion for the situation of the people living there at the dump. But I was also wrestling with questions about my current life in Canada. After all, I would return to a country with a higher standard of living than the people I had just met at the dump, and indeed, most of the rest of the world. I do not worry about where my next meal will come from. I can surround myself with all the latest gadgets our culture has to offer. I have leisure time, lots of it. North American life offers so many options unavailable or unattainable for many in the world like those residents of the Managua dump.

My experiences in countries like Nicaragua did challenge the affluence I am surrounded with. I have to ask myself about how this is affecting me spiritually. Is my culture enabling my faith or actually depressing it? Do I take most of my life of abundance simply for granted, forgetting any gratitude toward the giver? Can I consider myself "poor in spirit" when I have so much? Are people who appear to have so little actually better able to perceive their *need of God*?

### THE FACE AT THE GATE: LUKE 16:19-31

Jesus tells a parable contrasting a very rich man and a poor beggar named Lazarus. The poor man lay at the other's gate, hoping for some crumbs to fall from his table to satisfy his hunger. Both men die. In a reversal of what Jesus's hearers (and probably many today) might expect, the poor man is carried to heaven ("the bosom of Abraham"), but the rich man finds himself in the torments of Hades, the land of the dead. The situation is truly reversed in that the rich man cries out in the agony of thirst for Lazarus to come to his aid, to just dip his finger in water and cool his tongue. But that could not be, as there is established a chasm between the two.

Let us take a deeper look at that story as it relates to the first Beatitude. Jesus blesses the poor in spirit. To begin with, I caution against making overgeneralizations. Riches and prosperity by themselves do not necessarily block faith. The issue is with what those things do to our lives. Neither is poverty in itself a doorway to faith. Following mission trips that I have been on, I have encountered the remark, "Those people may be poor, but at least they are happy." Some are. However, many are dispirited, depressed, ill, malnourished, and bitter about their conditions. The church in Nicaragua where we were working had to have live-in guards; poverty also creates a climate of crime.

The man in the parable is defined only by the wealth that brought him status in life. Helmut Thielicke fleshes out this individual:

> People whose whole life is absorbed in their wealth have to frolic and regale themselves in order to prevent themselves from seeing that right next door to where they live there is another world, a world of the slums. Lazarus with his sores and filthy rags. So the rich man shuts his eyes whenever his carriage is driven through the slums. He can't bear the thought that this could happen to him too. For there would be nothing left of him if he ever had to give up his style of living. He is so utterly hollow that he needs at least this shell of wealth to keep him from turning into thin air…therefore, keep Lazarus at the back door, so he won't be seen![3]

The blessing of this Beatitude confers becoming a part of the kingdom of God. Discovering the Jesus of that kingdom means touching him in the face of those who are suffering and in need (c.f. Matthew 25:31-46). Considering the living reality of those of his kingdom whom Jesus gathered during his earthly ministry sharpens the focus of the parable. I have to ask myself: *Am I too much like that rich man, immersing myself in affluence and blinding myself to those like Lazarus suffering just outside?*

## CLENCHED FISTS

Jesus blesses the poor in spirit, those who can acknowledge their need of God. I would like for us to begin by exploring what it means to *not* be poor in spirit. Reflect on the following image. Stretch out your hands. Keep one hand palm up and open. With your other palm begin to clench your fist. Better still, find a small rock to wrap your hand around and tighten your fingers. With that clenched fist, I would like for you to consider all that you may be holding on to in your life. A clenched fist is one that is unable to truly receive from God. The following are some possibilities of items that may be denying your poverty of spirit through what you are gripping too tightly in your life.

*Material possessions.* Our economy is based on acquisition. There is a strong underlying assumption that the more you have, the happier you will be. There are line-ups for the latest development in technology, and those seem to come at an increasing pace. We keep our eyes on commercials to ensure that we will know what it takes to keep up. As you tighten your grip on what you have, ask yourself: *Am I in control of all my stuff or does it control me? What are my deepest desires? What do I feel I simply could not live without?*

Do you remember the "rich young ruler" who sought out Jesus and appeared to be ready to become a disciple (Matthew 19:16-22)? Until, that is, Jesus identified the hold this man's wealth and possessions had on him. When challenged to give it all up, give it to the poor, the young man sadly walked away. He just couldn't do it; what he had held him too tightly. How open are you to freely live as a disciple of Jesus?

*Status.* If I were to ask you to honestly tell me exactly who you are, would you respond by giving me your job, title, or degrees? Would you be able to describe to me the essential "you" whom God created? How tightly do you hold on to an *externally* established identity?

*Internal baggage.* Do old wounds continue to burden you and deny your true self? Is your fisted hand holding unresolved grief, wounds from the past, or negative vows spoken over you years ago? How free are you to truly live in the present without baggage from the past wearing you down?

*Self-sufficiency.* I remember one of those church children's stories often shared around Thanksgiving of a little boy who was asked to give God thanks before the big meal. He replied with, "I don't need to thank God, because my father owns the grocery store!" Do we not in our culture carry a feeling of self-satisfaction about how well we are doing, how much we provide for ourselves, how successful we are? It would appear that an increasing number of people feel that God is really irrelevant to their lives. They have all they need, thank you. How much of you is wrapped up in pride?

*Self-righteousness.* Perhaps the unease I felt regarding the remark about counting my blessings in comparison to the poor of the world is that it will not lead to gratitude or sharing what I have, but rather to developing a feeling of self-righteousness. Well, God has blessed me, hasn't he? I must be doing just fine, thank you.

Jesus gives a warning in his parable about the two men praying in the Temple (Luke 18:9-14). One, a Pharisee who diligently kept the law, prayed: "God, I thank you that I am not like other men—robbers, evil doers, adulterers—or even like this tax collector. I fast twice a week and give a tenth of all I get." It was the other man, a Publican, who prayed out of his need whom Jesus identified as the one who was justified in the eyes of God. There is an insidious sense of entitlement that can creep into our spiritual life that we grip on to. The danger, of course, is that true righteousness based on a living relationship with God and others is disabled by such self-righteousness. We will explore more about righteousness later in this book.

*Spiritual blindness.* The most telling aspect of the story of the rich man and Lazarus is that the rich man appeared to be oblivious of Lazarus, of the need lying at his doorstep. If he did notice, he did nothing to engage or assist the poorer man. Sure, I have been to third-world countries where it is impossible not to witness harsh poverty, but what about my own community? Am I clenching on to too much "me" to the point of ignoring all the "you" right around my own door? Are you?

**OPEN HANDS**

Let us now turn to your other open palm, and we will discover what it means to be "poor in spirit." Jesus is not advocating some sense of being "poor spirited," harbouring a false kind of humility. What he is offering is the blessing to be found in total openness to the presence of God in our lives, to serve the living Jesus and to be a willing vessel of the power of the Holy Spirit. Open hands indicates a willingness to pass through the narrow gate and embark on the more difficult pathway of discipleship. It is, as Jesus goes on to teach, to "seek first the kingdom of God and its righteousness" (Matthew 6:33).

The Greek word used for poor is *ptoches*, which literally means "to cower," implying almost complete destitution and total need. Our challenge is to fully open our hands in absolute need of what God in Jesus desires to bless us with. Consider the following aspects of having open hands:

*A proper assessment of everything.* If we can fully grasp the fact that absolutely everything that exists, including ourselves, comes from God, we will become gracious receivers of all his gifts. The fact is that ultimately we do not own anything. The biblical truth is that we are to be responsible stewards of what God owns that we share in our lives. That will provide a corrective to those closed-fisted qualities listed above. When Jesus urges us to seek first the kingdom of God, it was in answer to the level of anxiety people harbour about what they will eat or what they will wear. Jesus is not advocating poverty, just about establishing the right priorities in our lives. Seek first the kingdom, he teaches, and whatever else you need will be provided to you. Open hands are trusting hands.

*Value.* This leads to an authentic sense of personal value, which is an essential part of becoming poor in spirit. Make the following affirmation:

> I will value myself as a gift from God, unique and created with gifts of personality and ability. Therefore, I will not tolerate any abuse of such a gift either in myself or in another. Without fear of judgement, I will accept the reality of who I am not based on possessions, position, or another person's opinion of myself. I will be poor in spirit in order to truly realize the richness that God has created in me.

*Freedom from fear.* There is an underlying fear associated with our clinging to external factors such as status and possessions. What might happen if I lose what I have? What will others think of me if am unable to keep up my current lifestyle? Who will care about me if I do not measure up to the expectations of culture? A part of becoming poor in spirit contains a release from such fears. My needs are supplied by God; therefore, I do not need to slavishly seek the approval (or fear the rejection) of others.

*Need.* As we have been learning, the root of poverty of spirit comes from recognizing our need. This goes against much of our conditioning that we must be strong, self-reliant, and self-sufficient. Jesus can only bless us when we admit our spiritual need and open up our hands to receive. Remember the upper room scene just prior to Jesus's arrest (John 13:1-20). Seeing that none of the disciples took on the necessary task of washing feet, Jesus wrapped a towel around his waist and proceeded to do just that. Peter protested. This was not right, although obviously Peter had not offered to wash feet himself. Jesus quickly identified the self-pride that led to Peter's refusal. If he really desired to be part of Jesus's kingdom, it would be necessary for Peter to allow this loving servant act of Jesus. So must we. Pride must be broken to create a receptive spirit.

**WELCOME TO THE KINGDOM**

Consider again your two hands. As you unclench your grip on externals, as you recognize your need of a Saviour, as you prepare to receive a blessing, you are becoming poor in spirit. With open hands and a willing life, the blessing of the Beatitude will be yours. You are welcomed into the kingdom of God! Life in that kingdom is characterized by the lifestyle we will pursue in these teachings of Jesus.

We realize that this kingdom that Jesus proclaimed and initiated is unlike any other earthly kingdom. It is a gathering of all those who have entered through that narrow gate. It is the fellowship of all who are journeying the pathway of the

Beatitudes. It is a surprising kingdom made up of all manner of people: the ones to whom Jesus reached out, the ones who accepted his invitation. It is a kingdom of the heart, not based on any criteria other than a willingness to receive God's love in Jesus, a true poverty of spirit.

No castles and moats for this kingdom: it grows person by person by person. In that way it is extremely powerful, and its growth potential is unlimited. Think about how many earthly kingdoms and empires have come and gone over the millennia and how enduring has been the Christian movement throughout the world. Jesus likened his kingdom to a mustard seed that when planted seems small and insignificant, but which grows large enough for birds to rest on it (Matthew 13:31-32). The kingdom is without bounds as it permeates throughout all countries and cultures, like yeast, which silently yet powerfully expands (Matthew 13:33).

Get a life! Open up your hands and heart to receive the blessings God has for you! Welcome to the kingdom as you live these Beatitudes. God desires to fill your every need. Be blessed!

# HOLDING ON AND LETTING GO

3

*Blessed are those who mourn, for they will be comforted.*
Matthew 5:4

GET A LIFE! WE ARE EXPLORING THE INVITATION GIVEN BY JESUS to pass through a narrow gate and take up the more difficult pathway of life that leads to blessing. Part of that journey is an inward one, confronting emotions in our deepest being. The journey to blessing involves accepting, exploring, and experiencing those places of life that often we might rather not deal with. Unfortunately I have heard that "get a life" expression used to steer people away from talking about troubling feelings that cause discomfort in others. Truly, though, it is impossible to get a full life by avoidance. One of those places we must deal with is sorrow and grief. Here Jesus extends to us the invitation to mourn.

To mourn involves making yourself vulnerable. Grief is not comfortable. Perhaps that is why we so often attempt to cover over sorrow with superficial smiles even if our heart is breaking inside. Many of us at times have played what I term "hide and seek." We hide our true feelings in order to seek the approval of others. Different people have indicated to me feeling a sense of shame if they exhibit any outward show of mourning. We praise people who may be repressing their grief with, "My, how well she is holding up." Jesus counters all that by blessing grieving and mourning.

To deny grief and sorrow is ultimately to deny life. It is the first blessing of comfort to realize that Jesus clearly recognizes the pain of sorrow. The Greek word used in the Beatitude for mourning is *penthein,* which is a very strong word indicating not sentimental sadness but rather intense and intimate sorrow. I find it a relief to know that Jesus in this Beatitude is encouraging a full and healthy grieving. The first step always is for us to allow the full experience of mourning; this is what will unlock comfort. Otherwise we are simply left with a deep suffering that will go on and on and that we do not feel we can ever share with anyone.

To retreat from our own mourning also puts up a shield in accepting such grief in another person. If we do not receive comfort, how could we offer support to another mourning person? Being able to mourn enables the comprehension of another's pain. Nicholas Wolterhoff speaks of a "prism of tears": "Perhaps I shall see things that dry-eyed I could not see."[4]

A number of years ago I sat by the bedside of a young woman in the late stages of cancer. She realized that she was dying but was very open and honest about the deep internal struggle she was experiencing. She shared with me a fascinating sketch she had just completed. I still have it (see p. 18). In the centre of her drawing, she placed a young boy holding a large bunch of balloons. Because of that he is floating a few feet above the earth. However, the boy is not able to float completely free, for below him, grasping on to his shoelace and not letting go, is his pet dog. For this young woman the sketch illustrated her struggle with holding on and letting go, indicating that soon she, like the child in the picture, would be able to let go, free from the pain of her disease.

I have used that sketch in working with people dealing with loss and grief. Comfort is provided both in holding on appropriately and letting go when that is necessary. Let us explore those two dimensions of mourning to discover the comfort that is available to us. We will be blessed as we allow ourselves to mourn.

## HOLDING ON

Mourning is a process of incorporating the reality of the loss of a loved one into our lives, living with the pain of losing, and fashioning a new future without the earthly presence of that person. Erik Kolbell states, "Our salvation lies not in denying the inevitability of loss but in learning how to fold it into our lives, learning how to mourn, perhaps more importantly, how to *use* mourning."[5]

Consider how comfort is provided in the following aspects of holding on in mourning:

*Memories.* I have had the privilege of meeting with groups of individuals who are working through the loss of a loved one. During one of the sessions the participants are invited to bring in a special object associated with their loved one and talk about it. The memories are deep and rich as stories are shared kindled by that object. We laugh, and we weep. Memory indeed is a gift from God. Sure, there can be troubling remembrances that keep us awake at night. But there is also precious comfort in a rich store of memories, for they are what we get to keep.

*Pain.* It may seem strange to list pain as something to hold on to in order to receive comfort. The reality of loss is pain, sometimes acute. Initially you need to hold on to the pain of the loss in order to truly work through it. The best advice is to journey *through* the pain, not denying it but rather doing the necessary work of grieving in order to receive the comfort that ultimately relieves pain. Yes, there may be times when that pain must be dulled, but there can be a danger associated with a desire simply to numb *all* the pain away, which for some people can lead to the misuse of alcohol or drugs. Working through the pain of grieving does acknowledge the depth of your relationship with your loved one. I offer a word of caution. If the pain of loss is too intense and you feel that you cannot go on, or you have strong feelings of "just wanting to go and be with the deceased loved one," you need to seek the guidance and comfort provided by professional help.

*Ritual.* The proper use of ritual encourages healthy mourning. It enables us to experience deeper meaning that we can hold on to. It is interesting to note that at the time of Jesus there was allowance for public expressions of grief. James Howell points out:

> Around Galilee when Jesus lived, mourning wasn't so rushed, or so hushed. Mourners would literally tear the clothes off their backs. Right out in the open, mourners would scream out in agony, scoop up dirt in their hands and shake the dust onto the tops of their heads. No one tried to go to work, or to "stay busy." Friends gathered and they lingered over their grief for at least a week in this intense fashion.[6]

Today a funeral or memorial service can be a rich time of meaning. Tangible, lasting memorials can be developed such as planting a tree or enabling a bursary fund in memory. Lasting gifts provide you with something to hold on to, and they enable the essence of that loved one to continue.

*Intensity.* One cannot simply "let go" of a relationship. Even when people do feel they are moving on through their mourning, I caution them to be aware that there may come times of sudden intense re-grieving. For instance, a piece of music, a smell, a few words can bring about a flood of emotions. A birthday, wedding anniversary, or the anniversary of the death are times that can provoke renewed sorrow. It is impossible not to hold on to the associations those items bring. Those times provide opportunity to review your precious memories and celebrate once again the gift your loved one was in your life. That is comforting.

*Dreams and Visions.* It is not unusual for people to have sensations of the presence of that loved one, of hearing their voice, or of experiencing intense, vivid dreams. Usually those times bring comfort, often with a feeling conveyed that the deceased loved one desires those left behind to be okay.

## LETTING GO

Yes, there are aspects of loss that comfort us as we hold on to them such as deep and lasting memories. On the other hand, there are some aspects of grief that need to be released. Holding on to emotions such as anger or guilt will block your receiving the comfort necessary for your healing. Consider the following items:

*Letting go of false restrictions.* I mentioned earlier about the difficulty our culture appears to have with grief, leading to a temptation to bury sorrow rather than experience mourning. It can be difficult to resist those who offer false comfort by attempting to have you restrict your mourning. An example is the sentiment often offered to a grieving individual that "it is about time you got back to normal." I feel what is being

23

attempted by this communication is that it really is no longer acceptable to that person for you to express mourning. If you appear to be sad you may even hear, "Get a life," said to you but in a very negative and restrictive way. It is that other person who is not open to mourning.

The reality for a grieving person is that "normal" was buried with their loved one. The far more difficult task is to build a new future within the new reality of the loss. Therefore, let go of anything that might restrict your mourning. Realize that you need time and space to process your grief and enable healing.

*Letting go of anger.* Dealing with a terminal illness or the sudden death of a loved one often contains frustration and disappointments. You may find yourself in a position that does not seem fair. Your mind may search for answers as to who is responsible for this. Anger can emerge, directed at anyone you feel has let you down. For example, a doctor may have missed the diagnosis, a minister may have failed to visit and pray, a loved one simply could not provide you support. Anger can also erupt against God: "Why, Lord, did he have to die? I prayed so hard." Finally, some people discover they harbour anger against the person who has died: "How could you leave me in this mess?"

These strong feelings do need to be worked through in order to let them go. Perhaps you need to seek out forgiveness from the person you feel did fail you in your time of need. It may be necessary to approach the doctor or minister in order that they apprehend the fact they let you down. You are allowed to cry out your pain and anger to God. He does hear and understand. If you experience anger directed against your deceased loved one, it can be helpful to put all your feelings into a letter and sit down with it at the graveside and just let it all out. Often the best comfort and healing for these raw emotions is to participate in a support group. You will be pleasantly surprised at how many people are also dealing with such emotions.

*Letting go of guilt.* There is a "flip side" to anger. Answering the question of who is responsible can result in turning the blame onto yourself. Guilt surfaces as you begin to go through all those "if only's" or "should haves." Indeed in a time of crisis and stress, there will be many things that could have or might have been done. If only we could go back in time and change things, but we can't.

Don't beat up on yourself with what did not happen. Let go of that kind of guilt. Comfort yourself. Learn to say, "I did the best I could under the circumstances." Life is a learning process. Perhaps what you have discovered in your experience can be offered as healing comfort to someone else. There is one word of caution: some situations call for the comfort of a trained counsellor, if there is very real guilt such as with the individual who caused an accident in which another died.

## THE COMFORT OF THE SHEPHERD: PSALM 23

What has brought great comfort to me in my times of mourning is Psalm 23. Let us revisit that scripture. To begin with, the psalm presents a wonderful pastoral description of shepherding in biblical times. Shepherds were responsible for the care of one flock of sheep. During the night, sheep from many flocks would be settled in a common fold for safety. In the morning each shepherd would come and call out their flock. They would lead them to the surrounding hills where the sheep would find pasture and safe drinking water.

Later in the day, the shepherd would lead his flock back to the fold. However, as night descends very quickly, the pathway through the valleys would now be in darkness. Danger lurked, and the shepherd guided the sheep with his protecting rod and staff. Sheep safely back, the shepherd could rest.

We easily make a transition from sheep and shepherds to view this psalm as a description of life. Times when things are going well are represented by those green pastures and still waters. The psalm also recognizes the reality of darker valleys, including that of death. The shadow of death forms a powerful illustration of the experience of mourning. Dealing with fear, disorientation, and helplessness can feel very much like trying to negotiate your way through a valley in the dark.

The key to the psalm, of course, is the shepherd who guides and protects the sheep. Furthermore, the psalm portrays the shepherd as the image of God. God provides for us throughout our lives but particularly accompanies us through the most difficult of times. Despite how desperate we may feel at times, the shepherd is right there beside us, guarding and protecting. Jesus declared himself to be the good shepherd (John 10:14). It can be very helpful to visualize him as that loving, protecting shepherd walking with you in your darkest hours. What would you say to him? What tears might you share together? Feel his arms holding you, his strength filling your weakness.

The psalm contains another comfort. The journey does not end with the valley of shadows. The shepherd safely delivers his flock back to the security of the fold. Beyond the darkness of the valley will be the sunshine of a new day illuminating the pathway into the future. Grieving does take some time. However, new pathways will open up as the darkest shadows disappear.

Note also that Psalm 23 closes with a different image. Once the final journey through the valley of the shadow of death is completed, a new experience awaits. There is a table spread, anointing oil ready, goodness and mercy in abundance in the "house of the Lord forever."

Get a life! Blessed is your mourning, for the shepherd of comfort is with you!

# SPINELESS OR STRONG?

4

*Blessed are the meek, for they will inherit the earth.*
Matthew 5:5

GET A LIFE! I CAN RELATE TO THE PSALMISTS WHEN THEY CRY out about the apparent injustices of life. "I had nearly lost my foothold. For I envied the arrogant when I saw the prosperity of the wicked…surely in vain have I kept my heart pure…" (Psalm 73:2-3, 13). Powerful and evil people seem to prosper. God's people, trying to live a good and godly life, often suffer. That unfortunate reality continues to be played out throughout our world today. Is there any real future for the meek and humble? How in the world can we anticipate the meek "inheriting the earth" when the strong and powerful seem to have all the control?

Currently there is a focus on the issue of bullying, particularly amongst young people. Despite all the recent attention, the problem would appear to be accelerating with the more recent development of "cyber-bullying" over the Internet. Bullying is simply aggression. A bully attempts to bolster themselves by overpowering another, often seemingly weaker, individual. At one time it was felt that dealing with a bully was just another part of growing up. However, when a victim commits suicide, feeling that they cannot escape, it is a very serious issue.

Why do some people feel the need to overpower another person for their own gratification? We must realize that each of us wields power. It can be physical, verbal, or as we now realize, electronic. Words can cut and wound just as much as a physical attack. Putting down or ostracizing another can be devastating.

In bullying there is a victim. Too often we discover that bullying has been going on for some time before the victim admits to it. There is pressure to "just put up with it." Unfortunately, that often allows the aggression to escalate. I have read long lists of advice for parents about what to watch for if they suspect their child is being bullied, including: trouble sleeping, loss of appetite, fear of going to school or activities where other students are present, marked changes in attitude or habits, unexplained loss of personal items, or injuries that cannot be explained.

Now we are finding another critical link in the problem with bullying: bystanders. Research shows that in approximately 80 percent of bullying incidents others were watching or aware of the situation. It would appear that most children are uncomfortable with bullying, but in the past, very few would intervene or report the activity. Even worse are those times when bystanders join in the name calling or even physical attack on a victim. Being a friend to someone bullied can risk similar abuse. It would also appear that too often in the past authorities too just "turned a blind eye" on bullying.

In all of this we have an all-too-human situation. Aggression, on the one hand, does so much damage. Passivity, on the other hand, allows or even encourages that aggression. That brings up the biblical concept of meekness. It is too often wrongly described as passive weakness, spinelessness, or being the one to merely put up with what is wrong. That is simply incorrect. The Greek word for meek is *praus*, which is often used to describe the taming of a wild animal. Basically meekness is strength, but *under control!*

Therefore, our journey along the narrow pathway to blessing will involve a focused effort on our part to use our God-given strength and power to bring about God-intended good rather than allow it to get out of control and become destructive. Meekness develops from the Old Testament Hebrew word *anaw*. That term is used countless times in the Psalms to describe a person who in obedient humility accepts the guidance of God. In Proverbs, there is offered wisdom to the humble: "it is better to be humble and stay poor than to be one of the arrogant and get a share of their loot." (Proverbs 16:19)

As noted above with the illustration of bullying, we are capable of great strength *out of control.* Once again, clench your fist. There is a lot of power in that fist, and it can be used to wield great harm. Consider those times in your life when you have used your power and strength *against* someone else. It can take the form of harsh and critical words. It may be through more violent outbursts and at times may become abusive. As well, it can take the form of hostile silence or of cutting another person out of our lives. Out-of-control strength can result from *reacting* to the violence set off by another, sadly leading to escalation. Ghandi is reported to have said, "You start by taking an eye for an eye, and pretty soon the whole world is blind."[7]

The other extreme of passive acceptance of the wrong in this world is certainly not biblical meekness, and it is not right! That is not strength under control; it is no strength at all. In our example with bullying, it may take far more inner strength for a young person to stand up to a bully, to step in to stop the hurt, or to befriend a victim. That is what true meekness can accomplish.

Consider the greatest example of meekness, Jesus. His strength and power came from God and because of that could be formidable. Remember, however, his gentle compassion toward the ones who had been hurt, bullied, and abused in his time. A woman was brought to Jesus one day, accused of being caught in the act of adultery (John 8:1-11). No doubt that probably was the case; however, I have always wondered about where the male partner was in all this and whether this woman was "set up" by those religious authorities in an attempt to trap Jesus.

Whatever the situation, the Jewish law called for her stoning, and those religious officials and the gathering crowd were quite ready to mete out that punishment. Jesus turned that potentially violent situation back on the accusers: "Let the one who is sinless cast the first stone." Then with loving forgiveness Jesus released the woman—"Go and sin no more"—giving her a second chance at life. Jesus's meekness, his strength under control, saved her life.

Consider also the scene in the Temple where Jesus overturned the tables of the moneychangers (Matthew 21:12-13). In order to present a sacrifice, an offering such as doves had to be purchased. In the Temple precincts were individuals who would change the Roman currency of the street into the necessary Temple coinage to make the transaction. What they did was take a hefty cut for themselves, essentially extorting money from the people. Remember that many of the people coming to make offerings were poorer people such as Mary and Joseph. Where was meekness? It was there. Jesus was justifiably angry at the injustice being conducted in the house of God. His strength burst through, but it was directed correctly toward the changing of an unjust situation. Meekness means using strength as a blessing, not a curse.

## Psalm 37

Jesus's beatitude about meekness is drawn from Psalm 37, including the promise of inheriting the earth. Use that psalm to discover many ways in which you can begin to apply meekness in your life:

- We are not to fret or become anxious about evil doers, sapping our own strength without changing anything (vs. 1).
- We are not to envy them or attempt to duplicate their practices, seeking the wrong way to prosperity (vs. 1).
- Instead, we are to trust and delight in God, not comparing ourselves to those evildoers' success, but concentrating on the blessings God promises to us (vs. 3-4).
- Patience is essential to meekness, not giving in to momentary anger or thoughts or revenge, but instead seeking God's best for the long term (vs. 7).
- We are not to allow anger or wrath, for that is letting go of our control over our strength (vs. 8). We are to consciously depart from evil in order to do what is good (vs. 27).
- We must discover proper ways in which to bring blessings into the world: the righteous "are always generous and lend freely; their children will be blest" (vs. 26).
- We are to guard our tongues, realizing the power of words to bless or to curse. Meekness is uttering wisdom and speaking truth and justice (vs. 30).
- Despite what may be going on all around us, even if we are being hurt or bullied, God is our ultimate safe refuge (vs. 40).

- God will vindicate. Evil people appear to flourish now, but "like grass they will soon wither, like green plants they will so die away" (vs. 2). Essentially God is laughing at their proud pretensions, perhaps a good way for us to view the ultimately futile efforts of those who build themselves up by attacking someone else (vs. 13).

## INHERITANCE

The most intriguing aspect of this Beatitude is the promise that the meek will inherit the earth, which is an echo from Psalm 37: "But the meek will inherit the land and enjoy great peace" (vs. 11). Probably with a bit of humour some have indicated that once the strong and mighty get through with the world, who would want it? Just how will God's people, the meek, actually inherit? Allow me to suggest a set of "meekness affirmations" drawn from a variety of sources that may shed some light on this inheritance from meekness:

- In being meek, I give up the all-too-human temptation to compare myself to others. I will not become anxious, fretful, or envious of what someone else is or has. My security is in my faith in God and the living presence of Jesus through the Holy Spirit in my life. I will walk freely upon the earth.
- Therefore, I loose myself from the fear of not measuring up to some external standard or attempting to get ahead by putting someone else down. My identity is firmly rooted in God's assessment of myself as a valued creation. For young people, that means not allowing any lies spread over the Internet or even on the lips of a bully to take root. That certainly requires strength to withstand. Standing up to external pressures can really only succeed if you can affirm the value God has for you

and his divine plan for your life over anything someone else says.

- I will not allow my joy to be taken from me by those who might try to intimidate me, attempt to overpower me, or make me feel worthless. No matter what, my time on this earth will bring an inner contentment.

Jim Forest quotes an interesting Japanese saying: "The thief left it behind: the moon at the window." He goes on to explain that, "A burglar can strip your house of everything and even burn it to the ground. But a burglar cannot steal the moon—or your honesty or decency or capacity to love. A thief cannot deprive you of your faith or make you like himself."[8]

- In keeping my strength under control, I provide the opportunity for God's kingdom to grow.

Erik Kolbell puts it this way: to inherit the earth "means wresting a piece of creation that has been ceded to the demons and reclaiming it for God."[9]

- As meekness joins meekness, I will be part of a loving and accepting community.

James Howell makes an important distinction that the Greek word for meek in this Beatitude is not the single *praus* but is actually *praeis* (plural). "The meek isn't the single, lonely, meek individual. Generally, anyone with meekness is isolated, marginalized, and left alone. But Jesus uses the plural, suggesting there is a community, some sense of belonging among the meek."[10]

- This reclaiming of the earth for God's kingdom is an ongoing process of inheritance for the meek. Even though I may at times feel frustration and disappointment with the situation I am in, I will have the patience necessary for God to work out his will and purpose through my life. I realize that although the results may not be immediate, God is in control!

Giovanni Papini sees the meek in this way: "they are like water which is not hard to touch, which seems to give way before other substances, but slowly rises, silently attacks, and calmly consumes with the patience of the years, the hardest of granites."[11]

Get a life! Join the great company of the meek, who have their priorities right, their strength under control! Get a life as you inherit the earth and turn it into God's kingdom!

## ALWAYS SOMETHING MORE

5

*Blessed are those who hunger and thirst for righteousness,*
*for they will be filled.*
Matthew 5:6

GET A LIFE! I AM SURE YOU HAVE HEARD THE EXPRESSION "bucket list." I am not sure just when this phrase first appeared, but you may have considered making one. A bucket list is an outline of things to do or places to visit before you die, or "kick the bucket." There was even a movie made on this theme. I have never sat down and wrote out such a list for myself, but as those around me know, I do have many places yet to visit on this earth and lots of things I still dream of doing.

In looking at the bucket lists of others, I realize that out of some of the common items I have actually accomplished a few of them. I trekked the Inca Trail twice, the most recent time a great adventure with my daughter Sarah. I hiked from the South Rim of the Grand Canyon to the Colorado River and back—all in a single day! My wife, Lorraine, and I have completed one pilgrimage to the Holy Land and are eagerly anticipating a return visit. Other common items I have crossed off from further consideration: getting a tattoo (are you kidding?), climbing Mount Everest or Kilimanjaro (I had enough altitude challenge in Peru), or skydiving (don't think so). However, it is exciting to always have something more to accomplish, more to dream, yearnings to fulfil.

Does that same idea also characterize your spiritual life? Are you eagerly moving ahead, or do you find yourself living on a "plateau" of satisfaction with your relationship with Jesus? You may indeed need to "get a life" spiritually. This Beatitude of Jesus confers a blessing upon *insufficiency* rather than upon accomplishment. In fact, Jesus blesses a sense of "divine discontent" with the way things are based on a yearning for something far better. Unless we are truly hungry and thirsty for what he desires for us, we may be on the wrong pathway!

We are to yearn for righteousness. Let us explore that word. The Greek word used in this Beatitude is *dikaiosune,* essentially implying a right relationship with God. Such a relationship comes not from our effort but rather from accepting the gracious forgiving love of God in Jesus. In Paul's letters the word *dikaiosune* is translated justification. We are justified, made right with God, as we trust in what Jesus has purchased for us on the cross. It is through Jesus that we become righteous, that is, come into a complete relationship with God through him.

### Two Sons: Luke 15:11-32

There is a danger for us if we set our spiritual bar too low, if we accept much less than what God has for us. We often lose our passion for more. We fail to maintain our spiritual appetite. Let us walk through the story Jesus told about a father and his two sons.

To begin with, it would certainly appear that the father's home provided for both sons with a rich inheritance as well. However, the younger son entertained other cravings. Get a life? This boy dreamed of faraway places, exciting living, friends galore! When he had the opportunity, he demanded his share of father's inheritance and took off. Basically in that culture, by doing that he was declaring that for himself he now considered his father dead. A serious step indeed, but this individual had his sights set on far brighter lights than he felt were on at home

Think for a moment about your bucket list or perhaps the standard of living you aspire to. Does that take precedence over any spiritual yearnings? Do you feel that you have accomplished so much and acquired so much that you don't really desire anything more? Who needs God when we have so much? Have you or someone you care about "moved out of the father's house" seeking fulfillment far from there?

In a way, many in our culture are prodigal sons and daughters. When I visited Malawi in Africa this past year, I spent time visiting some very quickly growing Christian churches. In a conversation with some young people being trained as pastors, they raised some intriguing questions about their perception that spiritual life in North America was waning. I couldn't disagree. As long as the bright lights and affluent lifestyle of our culture continue, our need for God often is pushed to the back of our minds. Why does our affluence so often dull our spiritual appetite?

The younger son in the parable did have the time of his life…for a while. Eventually the funds ran out, the bright lights dimmed, the friends disappeared, and he was left destitute and alone. The realities of life sometimes do come crashing in upon us. The death of a loved one, loss of a job, the turning away of a trusted friend, family tensions, as well as the growing fears about the world around us can leave us feeling lost. Undernourished by a living relationship with God, many do find themselves like the younger son, resigned to his lot, cursing his fate and struggling for life as best he can. Finally, he figured out that it would be worth a shot to go back home and perhaps be taken on as a servant. Anything was better than his present situation.

A startling truth of grace is that God will honour even the most basic of our hungering and thirsting for a relationship with him. For like our heavenly Father, the father in the parable was eagerly awaiting the possible return of his son. He was willing to receive him not with judgement or condemnation, but rather thankfully with open arms to restore the relationship. It would have been expected in Jesus's time that a father, having been so humiliated by a son, would have disowned him forever.

This is the key to comprehending the depth of God's righteousness. The father in the parable goes against any and all rational or socially conditioned thoughts or behaviours. In fact, he lavishes the son with love: a ring for his finger, a robe for his back, and a feast of celebration to top it all off. This is so much like our heavenly Father. If we hunger and thirst for righteousness, be aware that God indeed has so much for us, an unending supply well worth our appetite for more!

### WHAT ABOUT THE OTHER SON?

In the parable there is another son, the elder brother, out there working diligently in the fields as he always has. News of the younger brother's return reaches him, and he is not happy. The noise of a great celebration getting going in the house infuriates him. No way is he going in! That brother should have stayed where he was, what with him wasting away the precious inheritance. The father came out to the pasture and pleaded with the elder brother to join in the celebration and welcome his brother home.

"Why did you never throw a party for me and my friends?" complains the elder. His father replied that all that he had was available to his son and always had been. The elder brother had never left home. However, he had never truly lived while he was at home. He had failed to fully accept his father's blessing even though it was there for him all the time. In his dutiful, hardworking existence, that brother had never hungered or thirsted for anything more than the constant routine of living. He missed out on so much potential blessing and settled for so much less than he was entitled to.

Too often we have bypassed this older brother in our focus on "the prodigal." Jesus, however, had something crucial in mind with this story. For amongst those who were hearing were the "elder brothers" of religion—those Scribes and Pharisees who contested much of Jesus's teaching. Like the older brother in the story, they were upset about this Jesus who associated with people they considered unclean. To them, that just didn't seem right. And like the older brother, they felt a strong degree of *self*-righteousness in their spirituality. After all, they had kept the law and all the required feasts. But in all of their dutiful religion, they had missed out on the joy of a true, loving relationship with God. They never had the sense to hunger and thirst for that.

Do not pass by this older brother or those religious leaders too quickly, for is there not a bit of us there too? That is, have we ever arrived at the place where we feel that we have earned God's approval of us? Do we not entertain some thought that we have put in loads of time in his service and that should *entitle* us to a blessing? Even more, have we ever allowed our spirituality or churchgoing to become a repetitious habit, like

41

that older brother slaving away day after day in the fields? Has our hunger and thirst for a real, loving relationship with the Father dried up with the routines of life or religion? Are we, like the elder brother, existing but not really living? Are we in danger of missing out on potential blessing?

Remember that the lavish, gracious love of the Father and the grand celebration is there waiting. We can, like the older brother, refuse to join in, feeling that we have not been properly rewarded for all we have done. The hunger and thirst of this parable is a challenge to the self-satisfied Pharisee and to any of us who do not crave more in our relationship with God. So, review again your spiritual life. Feeling secure and satisfied? Are you in danger of "staying out in the field" nursing your sense of self-righteousness? Beware, for Jesus's blessings are not offered for accomplishment but rather for hungering and thirsting.

### BEING FILLED

The promise of this Beatitude is that hungering and thirsting for righteousness will be met with God's supply, of being filled. The Greek word used for filled is *chortozesthai*, which implies being completely satiated. At the same time as we are being encouraged to maintain a life-long yearning for more, Jesus promises that our need will be met. As we open our hands to receive from God, we will continually enlarge our relationship with the living Jesus. We truly "get a life" on a continual basis.

The Bible often addresses God's provision for those who hunger and thirst for him. The Gospel of John records how Jesus produced the great miracle of feeding a vast multitude from a boy's small lunch of bread and fish (John 6:1-15). The crowd was fed, and that aroused even greater interest. The people followed Jesus, seeking more of the same miracle power. However, Jesus recognized that the crowd mostly wanted more to eat. "Do not work for the food that spoils," Jesus advised, " but for food that endures to eternal life, which the Son of Man will give you." Jesus alone will satisfy our spiritual hunger, for he is "the bread of life" (John 6:35).

Realize that as you hunger for righteousness, for that right relationship with God in Jesus, provision has been made for your filling. Feed upon the words of Scripture, use guides such as this or other books or resources, listen carefully to sermons that apply biblical truths to life, look up to role models of faith. Feed upon all that, and hunger for more. My wife and I share a love of discovering more and more about the Bible. A few years ago, Lorraine felt a desire to learn biblical Hebrew in order to grasp more of the depth of the Old Testament. She discovered the Hebrew teacher at our local Synagogue and enrolled us in an adult Hebrew class. She was right: learning a Biblical language enriches our understanding of the entire Bible! You need to hunger to understand more. You need to be fed!

John chapter four recounts a dramatic encounter between Jesus and a Samaritan woman. We are not sure just why Jesus and his disciples were travelling through Samaria, for Jewish people generally didn't go there. There was bad blood between Jews and Samaritans, which went back centuries. Despite that, Jesus rested by Jacob's well as a Samaritan woman approached to draw water. Jesus asked her for a drink. She was startled, for generally a Jewish man would not address a Samaritan woman.

Jesus then made a surprising offer to this woman: "living water." She assumed he was referring to drawing water from the well and that she would no longer need to come every day. Jesus meant so much more. But to enable this woman to receive the flow of spiritual water, Jesus first had to break through some layers of resistance in her. He requested that she go and bring her husband, knowing that the man she was with was not her husband and she had five previous marriages. Perhaps that is why she came alone to the well when other women would have come for water together early in the morning.

To receive the kind of living water that Jesus was offering, the woman needed to realize that she was *worthy* of the flowing, forgiving love of God. For a moment she deflected the conversation with Jesus by asking about where the true centre for worship should exist, an issue between the Jews and Samaritans. Eventually, thankfully, her eyes were open to take in that Jesus indeed was the Messiah. The offer of that flow of forgiving love was then truly received, and she hurried off to tell everyone.

Indeed, so many are thirsting for acceptance, an acknowledgment that God cares about them. However, many also harbour a deep sense of unworthiness, which, like the Samaritan woman initially, blocks the flow of the living water from Jesus. Perhaps there is something in your life blocking that flow as well. Realize again with this Beatitude that Jesus honours every request for love. He did not refuse a Samaritan woman with an iffy past. He did not deny Peter even after that disciple's three-fold denial. He will not deny you. Open your hands and heart to receive a refreshing, healing flow of abundant, life-giving love. God desires for us to receive his blessing. We must hunger and thirst for it, seek and desire it, and then joyfully receive all that the blessing entails. Be filled!

### HUNGERING AND THIRSTING FOR OTHERS

Biblical righteousness has a number of dimensions. There is the individual, as we have seen. But the right relationship with God also works out in morality, which extends to all people. God intends for all of his children to live a fulfilled life together. Our hunger and thirst must be not only for ourselves but also corporate righteousness made evident in mercy and justice for all. As we realize that conditions in our world cause great suffering due to injustice—where children are dying of malnutrition due to poor political decisions, where families are divided and forced to flee because of war—we should hunger and thirst for their healing.

Consider the prophets of the Old Testament. They pointed out the lack of spiritual appetite in the people made evident not as much in a failure to keep up the feasts and fasts, but more through the *un*righteousness of how they treated each other. Obviously their hunger and thirst for righteous living had become seriously dulled. Micah cries out:

> *This is what the Lord says: For three sins of Israel, even for four, I*
> *will not turn back my wrath. They sell the righteous for*
> *silver and the needy for a pair of sandals. They trample*
> *on the heads of the poor as upon the dust of the ground*
> *and deny justice to the oppressed.*
> Micah 2:6-7

Occasionally I hear people say that they have stopped watching the news because it gets them too upset. I feel that being troubled about the ills and evils of this world is a good sign: it means you haven't given up a hunger for something better or a thirst for healing love to flow. It means that your spirit is being called to pray for righteousness in the world and perhaps get involved in bringing its peace and justice into the world.

In 1995 when a Canadian boy Craig Keilburger was twelve years old, before heading off to school one day, he noticed an article in the morning newspaper. It was the story of a young boy Iqbal Masih in South Asia who had been sold as collateral on a loan his parents had taken out to pay for their eldest son's wedding. Iqbal ended up chained to a weaving loom for six years in a carpet factory in Pakistan. He finally escaped and began to speak out against the conditions of forced child labour. This unfortunately led to him being murdered. Reading the story in the paper kindled a hunger and thirst in Craig, who was the same age as that other boy.

Craig took it upon himself to rally his classmates to take up the cause of eliminating child labour. Craig even travelled to view the exploitation of children himself. He hasn't given up his hunger to, as he puts it, "Be the change." The organization he and his brother Marc began, Free the Children, is currently working in many countries, has built more than 650 school classrooms, and has spun off another movement, Me to We, which links Canadian youth to the needs of the world. If you meet Craig or Marc today, they are just as passionate, just as hungry for justice as they were those years ago.

Our quest for truth, justice, and mercy for all should be a constant hunger in our hearts. Our prayers for the redeeming of conditions that destroy lives should become our thirst. We know that God desires so much more. Furthermore, this hunger and thirst for others should become an incentive for us to redeem such situations and provide the healing of Jesus to the wounded and broken hearted right where we are. What situations in your community call out a hunger for redemption, a thirst for caring love? Where can you discover someone hungering for the bread of life offered by Jesus? Where might you meet a "Samaritan woman" thirsting for recognition, affirmation, and the ultimate forgiveness of Jesus?

Get a life! Maintain your hunger and thirst for righteousness. Realize that there is always so much more. Open your heart and life to the constant infilling of the Holy Spirit. Seek out righteousness where you live. Enable a right and living relationship with God through Jesus where you are. Be blessed!

# RECEIVING...AND GIVING...AND RECEIVING

6

*Blessed are the merciful, for they will be shown mercy.*
Matthew 5:7

GET A LIFE! IN 2007 MY WIFE, LORRAINE, AND I FULFILLED OUR
dream of visiting the Holy Land. We arrived in Tel Aviv, toured
Jaffa and Caesarea, travelled up Mount Carmel, and then spent
two days by the Sea of Galilee before arriving in Jerusalem.
Galilee is actually a small lake, but it is beautiful. We lodged at
a kibbutz guest house right on the shore. During the night we
could hear the sounds of fishermen out on Galilee. The next
day we had a boat tour on the water. Being on Galilee was an
amazing experience; for my wife it was one of the highlights of
her life (which is why we want to return and spend a longer time
there). It certainly was easy to imagine the many biblical stories
of Jesus that took place there. After exploring Capernaum and
the Mount of Beatitudes, we headed south along the Jordan
River, ending up at the Dead Sea.

As you journey south along the Jordan, the land becomes
increasingly arid until you reach the sea of salt. An interesting

lesson can be drawn from that geography. The Sea of Galilee receives water from Mount Hermon to the north and releases water through the Jordan River. That water flows southward to its destination, the Dead Sea. That body of water receives water, but there is no outlet, and so it releases none. That accounts for the high salinity as the water slowly evaporates in the heat. It is a reminder that life involves a necessary flow of receiving and giving. If you block up that flow, if you receive but do not give like the Dead Sea, your life will dry up. Galilee is rich in fish and surrounded by green hills and lush vegetation. Nothing survives in the Dead Sea.

This forms an essential aspect of Jesus's teaching regarding mercy. Both receiving and giving mercy must flow with his Spirit. One of the parables, "the unmerciful servant," provides a great illustration (Matthew 18:21-35). A king was settling accounts with his servants and discovered that one servant owed him ten thousand talents. This would constitute a vast sum, and it is impossible to conceive how a servant could rack up such a debt. The master demanded repayment. The servant begged for mercy, and miraculously, the king granted just that. Remember that this debt was astronomical, and it would strike Jesus's hearers as a bit insane for the king to wipe out that huge amount. The key for the parable is that the master did cancel the entire debt.

You might think that this servant, filled with a sense of immense relief, would be grateful for his reprieve. The story continues. On his way out, this first servant met a fellow who owed him ten denarii. That would amount to about one five-hundred-thousandth of the debt he had owed. However, this was an "unmerciful" servant, and even though the other pleaded for time to repay, he refused. The first servant received but was unwilling to give.

## RECEIVING

If we are to discover the blessing of this Beatitude, we must consider how well the flow of mercy is working in our lives. Remember our illustration of clenched fists and open palms. The unmerciful servant opened his hands to receive, then clenched them firmly and blocked giving. He was a taker, not a giver. He really had not absorbed the mercy granted to him by his master.

Let us explore the concept of mercy. It begins in a situation of inequality, of debt. You may have been hurt by another person and feel entitled to seek some form of retribution. You may have caused hurt to someone else, and they have the power of seeking potential retribution from you. It was within the full right of the king in the parable to demand total repayment of the vast loan or to have the servant and his family thrown into prison in a (probably futile) effort to exact some repayment. That would appear to be the structure of justice.

However, another dynamic is at work—mercy. If you have that power, or someone has that power over you to exact retribution and it is *not used*, then mercy has been given. In forgiving the debt the servant owed, the king was merciful. He was within his rights to take whatever action he required to have the debt repaid, but he simply cancelled it. In refusing to cancel his fellow's small debt, the servant was *un*merciful.

Jesus was deliberate in contrasting those two debts. We are to expect mercy from God. The Hebrew word used in the Old Testament for mercy is *chesedh*, and it appears countless times to refer to the nature of God. For example, in Psalm 86, the writer cries out to God for that mercy:

*Hear, O Lord, and answer me, for I am poor and needy. Guard my life, for I am devoted to you. You are my God; save your servant who trusts in you. Have mercy on me, O Lord, for I call to you all day long. Bring joy to your servant, for to you, O Lord, I lift up my soul. You are forgiving and good, O Lord, abounding in love to all who call to you. Hear my prayer, O Lord; listen to my cry for mercy.*

There may be times when we feel that the realities of our life are simply too heavy to bear. Remember the first Beatitude and the blessing that meets our need, our "poverty of spirit." The psalmist could be honest before God about being poor and needy. It is interesting to note that the narrow gate through which we are to enter to receive blessing is often that of our admitting that we are needy or sorrowful or heavily burdened. We cry out for mercy!

However, many continue to struggle with a level of unworthiness, of having lived in such a way that has built up a great debt against God. Just how much debt, how much of what you might have/have not done in your life might cause God to cut you off? Jesus was very deliberate in his parable. The debt the first servant owed was indeed immense and could never be repaid, ever. Yet it was cancelled. So, why should you think that God might withhold his love from you and not cancel any debt of life you have incurred against him?

The psalmist could cry out to God in confidence of receiving mercy and forgiveness, for that is the character, the *chesedh* of a loving God. Any debt incurred by us can be erased by what Jesus purchased for us on the cross. Mercy is totally available to everyone. Therefore, we do not need to be trapped by our past, restricted by our sin. Walking the narrow pathway of the Beatitude once we have unlocked the door often barred by our pride enables us to travel life in freedom. We are as alive as the Sea of Galilee, constantly refreshed in receiving.

## Giving

As that parable of the unmerciful servant so well illustrates, mercy accepted must flow outward from us as well; otherwise we wither. Again, that takes our worship of God far past any outward ritual to a true expression of the heart. The Old Testament Micah put it well:

*With what shall I come before the Lord and bow down before the exalted God? Shall I come before him with burnt offerings, with calves a year old? He has showed you, O man, what is good. And what does the Lord require of you? To act justly and to love mercy and to walk humbly with your God*
Micah 6:6-8

Note that Micah maintains a dual necessity: justice and mercy working together. Mercy does not consist of just "letting someone off" as if a wrong had never been committed. Justice is required to ensure that people are treated with equal dignity. Mercy tempers the requirement of justice with the act of love to transform the transgressor and redeem the situation.

Robert Wallace shares an old story to illustrate how justice and mercy can work together for good. Fiorello La Guardia, before he became mayor of New York City in the 1940s, served as a judge. During the depression, a man was brought before him charged with stealing bread, driven to that crime to feed his starving family. La Guardia was obliged under the law to fine the man ten dollars. That was justice. Then the judge took ten dollars from his own pocket and handed it to the court clerk to cover the fine. That was mercy. Furthermore, La Guardia "fined" everyone present in the court room fifty cents "for living in a city where a man has to steal to feed his family." That day forty-seven dollars was collected for the defendant.

That, according to Wallace, was justice and mercy hand in hand.[12]

The outward flow of mercy is essential to the life Jesus offers. Living out mercy before the outward rites and rituals expected by religion set him at odds with the Pharisees. They studied the scriptures, kept the law, and observed the feasts and fasts. But for Jesus, they more resembled the Dead Sea than the living Sea of Galilee. They received but had bottled up the offering of mercy. Listen to one of Jesus's admonitions to them: "Woe to you teachers of the law and Pharisees, you hypocrites. You give a tenth of your spices—mint, dill and cumin. But you have neglected the more important matters of the law—justice, mercy and faithfulness" (Matthew 23:23). In teaching the prayer we title the Lord's Prayer, Jesus adds an emphasis to our prayer to forgive as well as be forgiven. If we cannot forgive, the flow of God's mercy is blocked, and we really have not been able to truly receive forgiveness.

## AND RECEIVING...AND GIVING...

Which would you choose to be: the Dead Sea or the Sea of Galilee? The Greek word used in the Beatitude for mercy is *eleos*, which has the sense of pouring out, the way someone would pour out oil from a flask. Let us discover some steps toward maintaining the life-giving flow of mercy in your life:

- Make a list of all the ways in which God has granted mercy to you and the forgiveness you have received. Lloyd Ogilve reminds us: "Everything within us wants to bless the Lord because he can feel our pain in His heart and respond with unmerited favor for us, forgiveness even before we ask, forbearing our rebellion and sin, surprising us with fortuitous on-time blessings when we expect them or deserve them the least."[13]

Many of God's mercies you will have received through the gracious acts of others. Give thanks to God for that grace. Discover ways in which you can express gratitude to the one who gave to you.

- Now honestly consider again how open are your hands to receive mercy from God. Are there any old wounds that you are still clinging on to? Is there still pain that you keep buried deep inside? What do you need to release in order to fully receive the mercy Jesus offers? Receive the forgiveness that unblocks the flow of the Holy Spirit into your life.

- You will need to move beyond your rational self. There is a danger: our rational mind may cause us to entertain thoughts of being entitled to a need to nurse anger and seek retribution when we have been hurt. Somebody should pay! However, remember that biblical mercy is giving up that felt need to punish in order to maintain the flow of God's mercy. Have you ever felt: "After what she did to me, I don't think I could ever forgive her"? So often the hurts we harbour deep in our hearts, those items we are unwilling to forgive, actually cause us more harm than the person who had harmed us. As we go over old grievances and wounds, bitterness can develop that will cause great harm to us both spiritually and physically. Who do you need to forgive? From whom do you need to seek forgiveness?

- Discovering the flow of mercy outward is to include God in that equation. Later in the Sermon on the Mount, Jesus advises us to let go of the judgemental spirit in which we ignore our own faults (the "plank in our eye") yet pick out the failings of another (the "speck" in their eye, Matthew 7:1-5). We must prayerfully lift up the one whom we feel has hurt us and allow God's mercy to work in their life. Note that the Bible does not guarantee us that if we are merciful it will bring about a positive response from the other. However, the point is that it is our responsibility to extend mercy. Remember the necessity of maintaining the flow of mercy. A lack of mercy extended to others blocks our ability to receive the mercy of God.

- So often we must simply "let go and let God" deal with situations in our lives. James Howell points out, "Mercy frees me from the need to 'fix' whatever is wrong. Mercy is able quite simply to love, to be compassionate, whether the hurt is curable or not. Mercy can just stay with the one in need of mercy."[14]

Another writer reminds us that mercy may not initially appear to be fair. "Those who are merciful necessarily come up on the short end of the stick at times. If I am going to be merciful, I must be willing to lose; something must be more important to me than losing."[15]

- Brad Hambrick makes an important point in noting that mercy extended creates the possibility for redemption, and thus it must be extended no matter what. "Mercy is the willingness to accept personal loss for the good of another or for a worthwhile cause...if God is glorified, I am willing to surrender what I am due from someone who has sinned against me or lived foolishly."[16]

The story of Joseph in the Old Testament (Genesis chapters 37 to 48) is a powerful example of the power of mercy. Jealous of this younger and more favoured son, his brothers plotted to kill him but at the last minute relented and sold him to a caravan taking slaves to Egypt. Holding on to his faith in God, Joseph endured injustice and suffering in Egypt. His ability to interpret dreams came to the attention of the Pharaoh, and through that Joseph enabled the country to prepare for drought. He was made second in command to the Pharaoh, in charge of steering the country through the dry years.

During that drought, Joseph's brothers were forced to travel to Egypt and beg for food. Who do they stand before but Joseph? After all those years they did not recognize this now powerful administrator. But Joseph certainly knew who they were. This could be his great opportunity to get back at them for all they had done to him. However, he forgave them in a tearful reunion. His mercy maintained the flow of God's covenant to continue, for Joseph and his brothers were to become the twelve tribes of Israel. In God's hands, Joseph enabled the redemption of mercy!

The receiving and giving of mercy can have great power. The poet Yevgeny Yevtushenko shares a story that took place in Red Square, Moscow, in 1944. He was there with his mother when a column of twenty thousand German prisoners of war were marched through the city. The crowd looking on were mostly Russian women who had suffered through the war with Germany. Many had relatives killed—brothers, husbands, or fathers. There were clenched fists and looks of hatred from that crowd. Then, recounts Yevtushenko, something began to change in the watching throng:

> They saw the German soldiers, thin, unshaven, wearing dirty bloodstained bandages, hobbling on crutches or leaning on the shoulders of their comrades; the soldiers walked with their heads down. The street became dead silent—the only sound was the shuffling of boots and the thumping of crutches. Then I saw an elderly woman in broken-down boots push herself

forward and touch a policeman's shoulder, saying "Let me through." There must have been something about her which made him step aside. She went up to the column, took from inside her coat something wrapped in a colored handkerchief and unfolded it. It was a crust of black bread. She pushed it awkwardly into the pocket of a soldier, so exhausted that he was tottering on his feet. And now from every side women were running toward the soldiers, pushing into their hands bread, cigarettes, whatever they had. The soldiers were no longer enemies. They were people.[17]

Get a life! Continue to receive the mercy of God. Continue to offer mercy. Remember that mercy enables the power of God to work for good in any situation, giving both you and others "a life." Blessed are the merciful, for they shall receive mercy… give mercy…receive more…give more!

# HEALTHY HEART, PURE HEART

7

*Blessed are the pure in heart, for they will see God.*
Matthew 5:8

GET A LIFE! DOCTORS AND HEALTHCARE PROVIDERS CONTINUALLY keep us aware of the necessity of good heart health, of developing a lifestyle that will keep heart attacks from happening. You are no doubt familiar with these risk factors for heart attack: high blood pressure, high cholesterol, inactivity, smoking, diabetes, overweight, age, stress, etc. So far I am doing pretty well on that list other than age (can't change that) and cholesterol, which according to the blood tests at my last physical was a bit "up." I am now watching my diet more closely and increasing my physical activity. I spend my summers at a beautiful beach on Lake Huron where walking on the sand at sunset with my wife certainly helps deal with stress as well.

But now I want to direct you to another definition of heart, this time from the Bible. There are hundreds of references to the heart. Scripture points not to the physical organ beating in our chest but rather to the inner essence of our being. We often think of heart in an emotional sense, particularly on Valentine's Day, but the biblical heart refers to the totality of who you truly are. For example, Proverbs 4:23 states, "Above all, guard your heart for it is the wellspring of life."

When the prophet Samuel was commissioned by God to seek out the one who would replace Saul as king of Israel, he visited the family of Jesse (1 Samuel 16:1-13). One of the many sons in that family would be the chosen one. Samuel figured it must be one of the older boys, probably Eliab, based on his stature and appearance, tall and strong. God said "No!" Down through the rest went Samuel without finding the one God was indicating. After seemingly exhausting the list, Jesse brought in the youngest, David, who had been in the fields guarding sheep. And when David arrives, his destiny is confirmed.

God had cautioned Samuel, "Man looks at the outward appearance, but the Lord looks at the heart." Heart in this way confers a sense of character and identity, which God was seeking after in the next king. Despite David's weaknesses and failings, he is consistently referred to in the Bible as one "after God's own heart."

## HARDENED HEARTS

The biblical heart can also be in danger of disease. Moses went to Pharaoh to demand the release of the Hebrew slaves from Egyptian captivity, but Pharaoh consistently refused, despite the plagues, due to his "heart being hardened" (for example see Exodus 7:13). The prophet Ezekiel was given a vision of a restored nation and a renewed people. To accomplish this God would need to conduct some "heart surgery": "I will give them an undivided heart and put a new spirit in them: I will remove from them their heart of stone and give them a heart of flesh" (Ezekiel 11:19).

Beware of allowing your heart to become hardened and stony. Marcus Borg uses the term "closed heart" to refer to that condition and outlines some aspects of that. Just as you must be aware of the indications of physical heart disease, I invite you to consider whether your inner biblical heart is in danger of hardening:

- Blindness and limited vision go with a hardened heart. We will not see clearly when our hearts are closed. Enclosed in our own world, we neither see nor hear very well. We close in upon ourselves.
- A hardened heart is insensitive to wonder and awe. The world looks ordinary when our hearts are closed.
- A hardened heart forgets God. It does not remember the one in whom we live and move and have our being.
- A hardened heart lacks gratitude. If successful in life, a person with a closed heart often feels self-made and entitled, or if life has gone badly, bitter and cheated.
- A hardened heart affects the mind and one's reasoning ability. Wrapped up in yourself, your judgements will be based upon self-interest rather than concern for others or for God's world. Your own personal opinions will matter far more than listening to someone's feelings or thoughts.
- A hardened heart lacks compassion. Though it can be charitable, it does not feel the suffering of others. Thoughts like, "So those people are suffering, but they probably brought it upon themselves," may rattle around in a hardened heart.
- A hardened heart is insensitive to justice. If you feel you have enough to worry about without allowing any consideration for others, your heart may be hardening. [18]

## HEART PURITY

What then is a pure heart or a heart of flesh rather than a stony, hardened, closed one? The Greek word used for pure is *katharos*, from which we derive the word catharsis. The word means unmixed and clean, describing milk or wine that has not been watered down, or metal free from alloy. The word implies sincerity and integrity. As well, there is a sense of being purified, as in a cathartic moment. A pure heart, therefore, indicates a person who has developed unmixed motives, clear focus, and a single-minded purpose undistracted by all around.

In his Sermon on the Mount, Jesus made clear that his intention was not to do away with the Jewish law. It had served the purpose of erecting external standards of morality and behaviour that enabled a civil society to exist. However, external rules and regulations do not necessarily create the inner righteousness of the heart. Jesus taught that the righteousness of his kingdom must exceed that of the Pharisees who had carefully kept every detail of the law. Jesus is directing us to an essential inner purity of heart, of having pure motives and not simply obeying the requirements of the law. Jesus questions not only the outward appearance of sin, but also the inner root causes of that sin.

He offers some examples. The law based on the Ten Commandments clearly indicated a prohibition against murder: "Thou shalt not kill." Most of us would never consider committing that crime, but does that provide the total freedom of a purified heart? It does not. Jesus takes us to a much deeper place by pointing out how anger potentially creates bitterness, which is the pre-condition for murder. If we harbour anger in our heart, the hardening process has begun.

Simon Tugwell puts it well:

Jesus is insistent that his kind of morality concerns the heart. He is not satisfied with any merely external morality. It does not impress him that we should just manage to behave ourselves properly, he is not prepared to get excited about any observance of external purity… for him the important thing is that it is from the heart that good and evil proceed…we have somehow to get inside and unmuddy the source of life.[19]

## SEEING CLEARLY

The reward for purity of heart is vision. Again we are not thinking only of our physical eyes but rather of our spiritual being. Helen Keller is quoted as answering the question, "Isn't it terrible to be blind?" with this answer: "It is better to be blind and see with your heart, than to have two eyes and see nothing."[20]

We have discovered that having a hardened heart leads to restricted spiritual vision. A pure heart enables us to see the world in a new way, "with God's eyes." For many years John Newton captained slave ships sailing back and forth across the Atlantic Ocean. During that time on board he reports that he became increasingly depraved and uttered blasphemies against God. At his lowest point, he literally became a slave himself. In the midst of a terrible Atlantic storm, fearing his imminent death, John cried out to the God he had formerly denied. His prayers were heard, the ship docked safely, and John began a new life as a clergyman. He counted it all to the "amazing grace" of God to which he wrote a now famous hymn. "I once was blind but now I see" describes well how his change of heart clarified his vision. Teaming up with William Wilberforce, efforts began, which led to the abolishment of the slave trade.

A pure heart creates the possibility for us to receive the blessing of seeing God. Remember that we have been choosing that narrow gate and difficult pathway to blessing. How can I keep on that pathway and not be pulled away from it? It will require deliberate *focus*. I will need to keep my heart pure and my eyes fixed on God, upon his vision for my life. It will be necessary to move my focus away from the immediate circumstances that I find myself immersed in. I need a longer range vision to see above current difficulties and struggles.

Maintaining purity may appear to be "wimpy" in the cynical age in which we live, but it is far from that. I will side with purity of heart! I like how Simon Tugwell puts it: "Where cynicism sees through all that is beautiful and good and simple, to find murkiness within, purity of heart sees through ugliness and sin and pain and failure to find God within."[21]

Unfortunately life presents many disruptions and distractions. Consider how pure your heart is at this point in time, or how hardened it may have become (from our earlier checklist). Are the eyes of your heart fixed on God? Are you able to look out at the world and the people in it with God's eyes? Are you able to keep your vision *upward* on God, or are your eyes cast *downward* on the way things are now?

Some years ago I had to undergo some serious eye surgeries. I experienced a "torn retina" first in my left eye and then a few years later in my right eye. It was a frightening experience to suddenly lose my vision. Thankfully, due to delicate surgery, my sight was restored. Two years ago I had corrective surgery for cataracts, which also involved lens implants. Suddenly my former severe near-sightedness disappeared, and I now see clearer than I have for most of my life!

I wish there was a quick and easy surgery to correct loss of spiritual vision, to enable proper clarity in order to see God at work in my life and world. I also wish there was the kind of heart surgery advocated by Ezekiel, of replacing old stony hearts with new fleshly ones, the kind God desires. However, under the constant presence and power of the Holy Spirit, we can exercise that surgery upon ourselves. We can continually purify our hearts as we block out everything that would detract, interfere, or distract our focus upon God and his plan for our lives.

I was listening to a chorus, "Turn your eyes upon Jesus," and it got me thinking about our ability to see God. Would you like to see Jesus? Consider this: look in the mirror! Purity of heart will enable the living presence of Jesus in your life. Remember what Paul wrote to the Ephesians: "Your hearts and minds must be made completely new, and you must put on the new self, which is created in God's likeness and reveals itself in the true life that is upright and holy" (Ephesians 4:23-24). Are you able to see Jesus in your life? Do you need to pray for Jesus to transform your life into becoming more like him?

Get a life! We must continually purify our motives in order to retain a healthy spiritual heart. To continually travel on the narrow pathway of discipleship and kingdom living, we must keep our hearts, minds, and lives clear and strong. Lord, help us keep our eyes on you and not on present circumstances. Give us long-range vision of what we can accomplish for you.

# NURSING THE VISION

8

*Blessed are the peacemakers, for they shall be called sons of God.*
Matthew 5:9

GET A LIFE! A NUMBER OF YEARS AGO I WAS ASKED TO GIVE A talk to a local elementary school for Remembrance Day. In searching out something that would connect the concept of peace with a large assembly of children, I discovered the story of a Japanese girl named Sadako Sasaki. This girl was born in 1943 and lived in Hiroshima. As a very young child she survived the atomic bomb blast on her city. After the war she grew up as a typical child, running and playing. Unfortunately around the age of twelve, Sadako developed leukemia due to her heavy exposure to radiation.

During her hospitalization, Sadako was reminded of a Japanese fable. According to that legend, if a person folded a thousand origami paper cranes, their wish would be granted. Sadako began folding and hanging the cranes. She completed 644 cranes before she became too weak to continue. Upon her death, her school friends and family completed the thousand,

and they were buried with her. A statue of Sadako holding a giant golden crane was erected in her memory in the Hiroshima Peace Park. Sadako may not have had her dream of being cured fulfilled, but her story has inspired countless children around the world to carry on her vision of peace.

On the anniversary of the dropping of the bomb and on Obon Day, a holiday in Japan to remember one's departed loved ones, thousands of people gather to leave paper cranes near the statue. Following my sharing of her story with the children, they began folding a thousand cranes. I was invited back to view the entire assemblage of cranes hanging up and down the hallways of the school. Together we spoke the prayer that is written at the base of Sadako's stature: "This is our cry. This is our prayer. Peace in the world."[22]

That prayer for peace appears to be an eternal quest. It would also seem that those cries and pleas and prayers continue to be met with bombs, terrorism, threats, and innocent lives lost. Is peace just a vague dream that evaporates all too quickly in the harsh realities of our world?

## SHALOM

It is important in considering this Beatitude to begin with a true biblical concept of peace. It is a quality far beyond simply the *absence* of war or struggle. The essence of biblical peace originates in vision, the vision of *shalom*. That Hebrew word, which Jewish people use to both greet and bid farewell (and much in between as well), does not translate easily into English. At its root, shalom is a vision of wholeness, completeness, and full restoration. Shalom is the universe as God intends it to be, this world as it could function, totally healed and completely restored.

You can discover this visionary aspect of shalom in some key Old Testament prophetic books. Both the prophets Isaiah and Micah share the same vision of making war no more. In the age of shalom, people will stream back to God so that once again everyone will walk in his ways of peace. God will settle all disputes between nations and from this, "They will beat their swords into plowshares and their spears into pruning hooks. Nation will not take up sword against nation, nor will they train for war anymore" (Micah 4:3, also Isaiah 2:4).

This vision of shalom extends to all of creation, the totality of God's world together in harmony. Isaiah offers this aspect of the vision of shalom: "The wolf will lie down with the lamb, the leopard will lie down with the goat, the calf and the lion and the yearling together, and a little child will lead them...they will not harm nor destroy on all my holy mountain..." (Isaiah 11:6, 9).

Our task, simply put, is to maintain that vision and work toward bringing it into reality. The danger is to give up on the vision as being too utopian and hopeless in the face of so much constant conflict across our world. We are being called through this Beatitude to walk the narrow, difficult pathway of peacemaking, of bringing shalom into daily practice in all that we do. By joining forces with other peacemakers, we endeavour to make this world a peaceable kingdom. We are to become far more than peace-lovers or even peacekeepers, we are to make peace happen.

Perhaps the best expression of that task continues to be that wonderful ancient prayer of St. Francis of Assisi:

Lord, make me an instrument of your peace.
Where there is hatred, let me sow love.
Where there is injury, pardon.
Where there is doubt, faith.
Where there is despair, hope.

Where there is sadness, joy.
O Divine Master,
grant that I may not so much seek to be consoled as to console,
to be understood as to understand,
to be loved as to love.
For it is in giving that we receive.
It is in pardoning that we are pardoned.
And it is in dying that we are born to Eternal Life.

## BEATING BACK THE DARKNESS

To truly walk the pathway of peacemaking, we must keep our eyes fixed on the vision of shalom as lived out in Jesus. As we do that, we beat back the darkness of hatred and strife. Each peacemaking effort extends the kingdom of God, which is the kingdom of realized shalom on this earth. No effort to this end is too small or insignificant.

You may have heard the parable of the starfish. A boy walking along a lonely beach realizes that the sands are covered with starfish washed up by the tide. Since the starfish are still alive at that point, he begins to pick them up one by one and toss them back into the sea.

Along comes a man who stops and watches the child. "What do you think you are doing?" the man asks. "Surely you don't think you can make a difference. There must be thousands of starfish on this beach."

The boy simply bent down, picked up a further starfish, and flung it into the waves, saying, "Guess I made a difference for that one!"

We must not become discouraged about small efforts, for together we can achieve the restoration of shalom, often one act at a time.

We need only read further in Jesus's Sermon on the Mount to discover some practical personal applications of peacemaking. We are not to repay evil with evil, even it if costs us something. We are encouraged to "turn the other cheek." We must admit that it is very easy to respond to the harsh words said against us with our own voice of anger and condemnation. Our culture encourages us not to get mad but get even. Following the narrow road of peacemaking can be demanding. Jesus goes on to encourage us to go *beyond* what is expected. We are to walk the extra mile even when that is not expected. Surprise someone who may be hostile with an act of peace: it may soften their heart.

Furthermore, Jesus challenges the former sentiment that one should forgive a friend but not an enemy. In the kingdom of God we are to love the enemy and pray for anyone who has hurt or persecuted us. The goal is reconciliation, bringing together what sin has broken apart. We are called to enable healing in our own spirit, our family relationships, and where there are divisions breaking apart church or community. Attitudes and resentments divide. Only God's love can overcome and heal.

As children of his kingdom, we are to take the first steps toward reconciliation. In his teaching on dealing with anger, Jesus continues to counsel that before we worship, if we remember that a brother or sister has something against us, we are first to go and be reconciled with that individual. We must realize that in order to fully make peace, we may need to confront conflict and not turn away from it. We are not to simply "appease" a situation. Peace is not "wishful thinking" or pretending conflict doesn't happen. Peace at any price is not necessarily peace. No, to truly make peace, we may at times need to head directly into conflict in order to offer something better. It often is a risky business but it is necessary.

71

I have always appreciated the very practical advice for peacemaking offered by Paul in Romans 12:18, that we should endeavour to live at peace with everyone but with the proviso: if it is possible, as far as it depends on you. I am discovering that with most of the Beatitudes, in claiming the lifestyle of those Beatitudes, it must begin me. I am to take the first step. Paul goes on to offer suggestions about just how we are to take those steps in peacemaking: "If your enemy is hungry, feed him; if he is thirsty, give him something to drink" (Romans 12:20). It would appear that Paul is looking for the outcome that it would bring self-judgement on the part of the enemy and hopefully change in that individual (heaping burning coals on his head). I would rather see our peacemaking as the effort to transform an enemy into a friend. Are there opportunities in your life to be the agent of that kind of transformation by making an initial offer of peace and reconciliation? In that way, we are working toward "overcoming evil with good."

Jesus declares that peacemakers are indeed living as his sons and daughters. I rejoice on receiving news of the efforts of peacemaking children of God throughout the world. An example is being brought about through the efforts of "restorative justice." Based on biblical principles of peacemaking, this process involves bringing together the victim of a crime and the perpetrator. The goal is to enable forgiveness and reconciliation. I have heard some remarkable stories, particularly through the efforts of a Canadian organization, JustEquipping, working in Rwanda. That African country was torn apart eighteen years ago in an incredibly brutal and bloody conflict between two tribes. Hundreds were butchered.

JustEquipping meets with prisoners who have been convicted of some of those horrible crimes and then attempts to connect them with the families of those whom they brutally murdered. It is a daunting task, but case by case it is happening. During "Mission 7" to Rwanda in 2012, a report is given about one of those efforts. Two chaplains took a letter from an offender that contained a clear description of the victim and the attack and traveled to seek out the remaining family member. After much effort they found that individual, Onesime. His family had been wiped out by the offender who sent the letter. This is the report of what occurred following the reading of the letter to him:

> Onesime then takes the letter and looks it over himself before throwing it down. He sits down on the ground and pulls his coat over his head. Then slowly the sobbing and shaking starts…sometimes half an hour can go by before one of the chaplains is able to ask if he would like to talk about it. Onesime slowly reveals that for 18 years he thought someone from the neighbouring hill had killed his family. Now he has discovered that it was a young man that his family had taken in as one of their own. Even though he was not a Tutsi, they never thought he would betray them as they had loved him as a son. Onesime had also just discovered that his youngest son, three years old, had run in fear to a neighbour. She sheltered him until the offender came and demanded that he be turned over to the gang. He then picked him up by the legs and swung him against a tree until he died.

The chaplains listened to more of his story then prayed with Onesime. They ask if he would like to meet the offender. Onesime wants to try to forgive, to achieve his own healing. He would like to discover where the bodies of his wife and children were buried. He agrees. The JustEquipping representatives continue their report:

> Onesime's journey of healing has begun. It is far from over. There are many challenges ahead, many trips, expenditures, disappointments and stress. We, however, know that he is already a stronger man than he was that morning. We have seen over and over the power of forgiveness and healing, the new capacity to move on, the possibility of peace in the farthest corners of this land beloved by God. Now the chaplains must return soon to the prison and report back to the offender. He will be overjoyed if the victim agreed to receive his letter, devastated if he did not.[23]

JustEquipping has delivered two hundred such letters from that prison and has been asked to take three hundred more. The darkness of evil is being beaten back with the vision of shalom and the forgiveness of Jesus, one letter at a time.

Teachers are also peacemakers and therefore at risk in many parts of the world. As I am writing this, a fourteen-year-old Pakistani girl is recovering from being shot in the face point blank simply for promoting education for girls like her. In a large part of the world the realization is growing that the solution to violence and poverty is through education, particularly of girls. It will require the courage of countless individuals to stand against the powers that would deny them.

I met peacemaking children of God during a recent trip to Malawi, Africa. Peacemaking, bringing about shalom restoration and wholeness, takes many forms in that country. The efforts of the Church of Central Africa Presbyterian carry the good news of the gospel through bringing about hope in many forms. I toured a village in which a new deep well had been completed to bring safe water to the people. Deaths this year from cholera had disappeared. In the same village more sustainable agricultural practices are being introduced to provide food security, especially in an area hit hard by recent droughts and climate change.

Malawi has also been devastated over the past two decades by HIV/AIDS. The sad result is a vast number of children left vulnerable due to the death of parents. In some cases they are being raised by grandparents or other relatives. That presents a challenge for families with too many mouths to feed properly. Some AIDS orphans are abused by the relatives with whom they must live. There are many cases of an older sibling taking over the raising of younger brothers and sisters. Finally, there are children who have simply been abandoned. I visited Apatsa School, which was developed to primarily educate such vulnerable children and so to provide them an opportunity for a better life.

In eastern Malawi, out of the Mulanje Medical Mission hospital is the developing Uchembere network. Village by village, health workers are seeking to better enable maternal health. The death rate for babies and mothers following difficult births had previously been high. Again, hope is being offered. Malawi is just one example of some incredible work being done around the world in bringing the vision of shalom, healing, and wholeness into reality.

Yes, the daily news can be grim as we tend to focus on the hotspots of the world. Let us rejoice with the countless peacemakers who are making such a difference. In what ways can you become a shalom-living peacemaker right where you are? Ask yourself: *How can I live out the task of peacemaking in all the relationships in my life?*

Get a life! In your church, your community, or your world, explore the ways in which the darkness is being beaten back. Discover peacemakers diligently bringing in the kingdom of God all around you. Where can you join together with your brothers and sisters to bring in the kingdom of God? Get a life... as you discover the joys, and yes, the challenges, of peacemaking as the children of God.

NOT ALWAYS EASY

9

*Blessed are they who are persecuted because of righteousness,*
*for theirs is the kingdom of heaven.*
*Blessed are you when people insult you, persecute you*
*and falsely say*
*all manner of evil against you because of me.*
*Rejoice and be glad, because*
*Great is your reward in heaven,*
*for in the same way they persecuted*
*the prophets who were before you.*
Matthew 5:10-12

GET A LIFE! IN THE SPRING OF 2000, MY WIFE, LORRAINE, and daughter Sarah and I spent three weeks in Kiev, Ukraine, visiting the family of a young woman who had lived with us in Canada for a year. Kiev is a fascinating city, parts of which date back centuries. Despite initial language challenges, we soon learned to negotiate the transit system and got out to explore. The highlights were some of the Orthodox churches we toured.

One day we discovered St. Michael's Monastery Cathedral in the older section of the city. It is called the "golden domed" church, for it has soaring golden domes above the beautiful blue exterior walls. Once inside, we learned some fascinating history. The original church on the site dated back a thousand years to the founding of the Orthodox faith in Ukraine. The first cathedral church was built around 1108, seriously damaged in the Mongol invasion of 1240, and significantly restored in 1496. An equally beautiful bell tower was constructed around 1719.

However, during the twentieth century times became difficult both for Ukraine and for Orthodox Christianity. Communism and official atheism prevailed. During the 1930s, Stalin decided that the location where the Cathedral stood would be an ideal place for the administration buildings for the Ukrainian Soviet Socialist Republic of the time. The cathedral of St. Michael's with its soaring golden domes was torn down and a parade square put in its place.

Years went by, and in 1991 the Soviet Union fell. Plans began shortly following that to rebuild St. Michael's exactly on the original plans. It was rededicated on May 30, 1999. And so, the cathedral we entered in 2000 which looked so ancient was actually brand new. In fact, the interior frescoes and mosaics were still being installed at the time. The scaffolding we saw and presumed was for repairs was actually enabling the completion of the church.

What was most significant to us was the realization that throughout the twentieth century, through communism and the Nazi invasion of the Second World War, the Orthodox Christian faith, though attacked and persecuted, did not die out. We were told that the keepers of the faith during those times were the "babushkas," the older women who never gave up maintaining the faith and what churches remained. Thanks to them, Orthodox Christianity now is experiencing a revival, as many churches like St. Michael's are being rebuilt or restored. St. Michael's today is a fully functioning church and monastery thanks to those faithful who withstood years of persecution and hardship.

## NARROW GATE, DIFFICULT PATHWAY

Remember how we began our journey through these Beatitudes of Jesus. We responded to his invitation to enter through a narrow gate and travel a challenging pathway rather than choose the wider and easier-looking alternative. Our invitation was to fully experience life rather than risk the destruction waiting in that other way. The warning was made clear: the pathway of Jesus, though bringing blessing, would not be easy. In this Beatitude we discover that while we might rather not have to face persecution in taking up the way of Jesus, it is a reality facing us.

Hardships, suffering, and persecution can attack us from all sides, attempting to pull us away from maintaining our journey with Jesus and deflecting our focus upon the ultimate goal of establishing the kingdom of God. Jesus honestly includes in this Beatitude a blessing that comes not through achievement, but rather through withstanding persecution.

We would rather have it be otherwise, but any reading of the New Testament brings the realization that living out one's faith does risk being ignored, insulted, and so much more. James Howell puts it well: "Why should we expect to find ourselves in sync with a world that is so out of sync with God? As we sort through what the Beatitudes mean for us today, we need to pause, take a deep breath, and reflect on the truth: if we absorb Jesus' words, if we walk in his way, if we try to embody his words and stick closely to him in the real world, we will suffer."[24]

The Book of Acts is the story of the early years of the expansion of the gospel of Jesus outward into the world. There are many references to the persecution of the developing church. During his second missionary journey, the apostles Paul and Silas visited the city of Philippi (Acts 16). There Paul met with a group of women who gathered by the river, and from that a congregation would grow. During Paul's stay in the city, a slave girl began to follow him, a girl who had a spirit by which she predicted the future. For some days she persisted with this and called out that Paul and his company were "servants of the Most High God." Troubled by all this, Paul turned to her and cast out the spirit.

However, the slave girl's owners, who had used her spirit for their own profit, were distressed at their sudden loss of easy income. They grabbed Paul and Silas and dragged them before the authorities in the marketplace, decrying that "these Jews are throwing our whole city into an uproar." A gathering crowd joined in with the result that Paul and Silas were stripped, beaten, and thrown into the inner sanctum of the local prison, locked securely in stocks. There was a serious cost to being an apostle of Jesus in those days. There still is.

Stories of persecution within our worldwide Christian family unfortunately continue to come in. Churches are being bombed and burned. Worshippers have been murdered. There are places on earth where it is a high risk to wear a cross. Like the early Christians gathering in Roman catacombs to avoid attack, small groups of Christian continue to meet secretly and courageously worship together.

Max Lucado gives the example of Xu Yonghai, a Christian in China who worked toward the legalization of house churches.

For his efforts the government imprisoned him in an eight-by-eight cell with no toilet, only a tap for water. "My cell was the last stop for prisoners sentenced to die," he said. "At times there were as many as three other prisoners in the tiny, damp room, awaiting their date with the executioner." This persecuted Christian survived through prayer, meditation, and writing. With a bar of soap, he wrote out the key points for a book about God on the cell wall. Thankfully Yonghai was eventually freed and his book *God the Creator* has been published.[25]

In a somewhat lesser but still significant way, there would appear to be a growing opposition to Christianity in North America as Christian symbols and practices, such as prayer, are being removed from public places. Young people report that faith is put down at school even by teachers. Perhaps you too have encountered such opposition or at least the pressure to simply not talk about being a Christian even within your own family circle.

There is a constant temptation for us to want to avoid persecution, to rather choose the wider, more comfortable just-go-with-the-flow-of-culture pathway. Maybe it would just be easier to simply keep our faith private within ourselves, but that would be a denial. I think that G. K. Chesterton had a point when he noted, "The Christian ideal has not been tried and found wanting; it has been found difficult and left untried."[26]

On the other hand, it is important not to "romanticize" persecution and make it an end unto itself. That is, although the gospel and the cross of Jesus may be an offense to many as the Bible states, it does not help that gospel if we use it to offend others. We are not proven by looking for persecution. Being arrogant or abusive or forcing faith on others may result in persecution, but that is not what Jesus meant in this Beatitude. Peter in his first letter reiterates the blessing to be discovered in the midst of persecution but also warns that some kinds of suffering are not blessed. "If you suffer, it should not be as a murderer or thief or any other kind of criminal, or *even as a meddler*. However, if you suffer as a Christian, do not be ashamed, but praise God that you bear that name" (1 Peter 4:14-16, my italics).

It would seem to me that one of the greatest threats to living out of faith for us is not the actual reality of persecution but simply the fear of opposition. We do have an inner drive toward comfort, and at times this can lead us away from taking the risks of fully living for Jesus. We need to open that narrow gateway into the kingdom of God and face such fears in order to claim those blessings of God. Jim Forest puts it well: "What keeps us from the beatitudes is fear—fear of others, fear of the contempt of our peers, fear of being a social castaway, fear of poverty, and ultimately, fear of death."[27]

Being willing to follow the pathway to places of suffering and potential conflict, even rejection, is to accept Jesus's invitation to take up the cross and follow him. Living *for* Jesus will also involve living *like* Jesus, facing the same kinds of challenge as he did here on earth. That can mean literally risking your life. Throughout history, followers of Jesus have discovered strength to withstand suffering and challenge in this sense of identifying oneself with Jesus. We often wear a cross as jewellery, but we may be called upon to truly bear that cross with our total lives.

N. T. Wright describes it this way:

> If we are to be kingdom-announcers, modeling the new way of being human, we are also to be cross-bearers. This is a strange and dark theme that is also our birthright as followers of Jesus. Shaping our world is never for a Christian a matter of going out arrogantly

thinking we can just get on with the job, reorganizing the world according to the same model we have in mind. It is a matter of sharing and bearing the pain and puzzlement of the world so that the crucified love of God in Christ may be brought to bear healingly upon the world at exactly that point…Because, as he himself said, following him involves taking up the cross, we should expect, as the New Testament tells us repeatedly, that to build on his foundation will be to find the cross etched into the pattern of our life and work over and over again.[28]

## REJOICING

Earlier in this chapter we left Paul and Silas shackled in the stocks of a Philippian jail. In his Beatitude on persecution, Jesus tells us that in the midst of persecution we are to rejoice and be glad. It would seem that in the dank, dark, and dangerous situation these missionaries were in, unfairly accused and unjustly imprisoned, we might discover them sulking in a corner of the cell determined to never let this kind of thing happen to them again. *Lord, where are you? After all we have done for you, is this how you treat your servants? Couldn't things go just a little easier for us?*

Well, thankfully, none of those thoughts crossed Paul's mind. We discover that in that cell at midnight, Paul and Silas are rejoicing! Locks and shackles did not prevent them from praying and singing praise, while the other prisoners listened in, probably in amazement. What a place for worship! That is the key, actually. Praise and prayer will release faith and joy *within* any situation you may find yourself in.

This ability to rejoice even in great trouble and persecution is an enduring strength of faith. It brings the presence of Jesus through the Holy Spirit to us right where we are. Sure, life is not always easy, but this Beatitude offers the blessing of the constant presence of God no matter what is happening. Paul had to stand on that promise time and time again. Despite all of the intense persecution he endured for the gospel, Paul could maintain the strength of faith. He testifies to this in his letter to the Romans:

*Who shall separate us from the love of Christ? Shall trouble or hardship or persecution or famine or nakedness or danger or sword? For as it is written, "For your sake we face death all day long, we are considered as sheep to be slaughtered." No, in all these things we are more than conquerors through him who loved us. For I am convinced that neither death nor life, neither angels nor demons, neither the present nor the future, nor any powers, neither height nor depth, nor anything else in all creation will be able to separate us from the love of God in Christ Jesus our Lord.*
*Romans 8:35-37*

That is a declaration worth remembering any time we feel attacked, put down, or made fearful because of living out our faith. I am sure that throughout the world today countless Christians are taking heart to risk their lives for Jesus by standing upon affirmations such as Paul's.

Finally, this Beatitude is the only one of the eight that mentions a future reward as well as the earthly blessings we realize now. Jesus's blessing to the persecuted, the blessing of rejoicing, also contains the promise that "great is your reward in heaven." Therefore, keep the faith, hold fast to your journey along that pathway of faith, and be empowered to stand up to any opposition that you meet. Your eternal destination is assured!

Get a life! I will close with a piece of poetry attributed to Mother Theresa. Although it is felt that it had been passed on to her from another source, she had it pinned to the wall of her room. Here is the version I have:

People can be unreasonable, illogical, and self-centered, love them anyway!

If you do good, people may accuse you of selfish, ulterior motives, do good anyway!

If you are successful, you win friends and true enemies, be successful anyway!

The good you do may be forgotten tomorrow, do good anyway!

Honesty makes you vulnerable, be honest anyway!

What you spent years building may be destroyed overnight, build anyway!

People really need help but may attack you if you help them, help people anyway!

Give the world the best you have and you may get kicked in the teeth, give the world the best you've got anyway!

# EPILOGUE: DRIVER OR PASSENGER?

My study of Jesus's Beatitudes that led to this book has reinforced a number of things for me. First of all, these eight seemingly simple blessings are anything but that. Jesus invites us to step through the narrow gate and take up the pathway of discipleship. That pathway leads us to confront many essential aspects of our humanity, and this process does involve some struggle. The other broad pathway to simply "get by" in life, "going with the flow" attracts many but is ultimately unfulfilling.

Initially the places of blessing may have been surprising to anyone well established in our culture. Rather than extending a blessing to the powerful and successful, Jesus identifies the poor in spirit, the sorrowing, the meek and persecuted as worthy of his kingdom. I do hope that this study of those Beatitudes has created in you a "hunger and thirst" for discovering more of who you are in Jesus, of living more and more in his (and not the world's) kingdom, and of seeking a deeper relationship with God.

Also, immersing myself in the Beatitudes reinforced a fundamental truth of Christianity, that it is not a "spectator sport." If we are to live out those eight blessings, we must invite Jesus into every aspect of our lives, from mourning to living mercifully to peacemaking. Receiving such blessings changes our lives, making us more alive. It brings us together with others who have also opened the narrow gate to becoming full disciples of Jesus. Note that many of the Beatitudes bless us through our becoming part of the kingdom of God as his sons and daughters. God in Jesus makes us family with those others striving to live with mercy, making peace and enduring persecution at times.

Talk about getting a life! Discipleship under the blessings of the Beatitudes calls us to a higher level of living, both within ourselves and outwardly into our world. We have rejected the broad pathway of just getting by. We have chosen to fully get a life. We are committing ourselves to offering the blessings of God to everyone. We are no longer just along for the ride in life!

I like the illustration of drivers and passengers. When we were younger, we spent our time in vehicles as passengers. Once we hit the teen years, we wanted to move over into the driver's seat. Passengers do not have the responsibility for the vehicle. I see that as an example of what Jesus termed as the broad pathway. However, it is another matter when you drive. Tim Elmore remembers what he said to his daughter Bethany when she was learning to drive:

> So far, all your life has been as a passenger. You've been able to let your mind wander, to change CDs in the player, locate new radio stations, sing, shout, laugh and get distracted to your heart's content. Why? Because you're just along for the ride.

This is a caution for us. Are you content to just be a passenger in life? Before you answer no, consider the following questions. Do you blame others for anything that goes wrong? If things do go amiss, do you count on someone else to come and rescue you? Do you rely on someone or something to bring you happiness? Are you continuing to pin all your hopes on externals such as status, wealth, a level of defined success, or comfort? How easily do things around you cause you to become anxious and upset?

I return to Tim's lecture on driving to his daughter:

Things are different now. It's not that the ride won't be fun—it's just that "fun" isn't the goal anymore. You are a driver now. The steering wheel is in your hands and so are the rest of the passengers in the car. Both the machine we call an automobile and all the humans on board are at your mercy...you are the one responsible for getting to the destination. You are a driver now.[29]

Becoming a driver rather than being a passenger strikes me as a great illustration of what I mean by stepping up to the discipleship of the narrow gate, of truly seeking to follow the profound teachings of Jesus found in the Beatitudes. Our hearts more and more become purified, our vision more focused. We are not afraid to express deep sorrow or to risk making peace. We are freed from our need to prove ourselves to others and can open up our deepest fears and failures to God and accept healing and forgiveness. Persecution can no longer back us down. We realize our strength but place it under God's control. Empowered by the Holy Spirit, our lives become a blessing to others. We are in the driver's seat!

Continue to read further past the Beatitudes into the Sermon on the Mount. Jesus follows those Beatitudes with two illustrations. We are to be light to the world. Our lives are to give glory to God in everything we do. And like salt, we are to become a seasoning force, influencing all around with the presence of Jesus. Get a life! Jesus is offering you just that. Be blessed!

I would like to conclude this book by offering you a prayer based upon the Beatitudes that I wrote some years ago. I realize that as I journey through the narrow gate and up the pathway of discipleship and blessing, I will need to continually keep myself reinforced in my relationship with Jesus, who leads me onward.

Almighty God, today I choose to truly get a life. I open the gateway to discover the blessings you have prepared for me.
God of all wisdom, enlighten my pathway. Flood my life with the light of the living Jesus, Light of the World, so that I may see myself through his eyes.
Inspire me with the truth of my being. May I be honest and direct with who I truly am, apart from appearance, image, or pretensions.
Give me courage to face my true self. Give me assurance of the gentleness of Jesus who accepts me as I am. Lord, I admit my need of you. Fill me, Lord.
Cry with me, caring Jesus, when I am hurt. Dwell with my tears of deepest sorrow.
Bless the tears I share with those around me when they are wounded and struggling.
Comfort me, loving Jesus, when I mourn.
Steady me, Lord, when I allow my emotions to overwhelm me.
Still my voice when I am in danger of speaking words of condemnation or rage.

Help me to control my actions when they might
cause harm.
Lord, I know I will experience strong feelings, but
keep me meek.
Gentle Jesus, encourage me to be kind to others.
Strong Jesus, enable me to stand firm against what is
wrong in my world.
Lord of perfect will, be with me as I live in this very
imperfect world.
Challenge me when pleasure or comfort diminishes
my relationship with you.
Bless my hunger and thirst for a deeper relationship
with you.
Bless my yearning for justice and peace for all your
children.
Keep me restless in desire to bring in your kingdom
of grace.
Merciful Jesus, you stretched out your arms on the
cross and gave yourself for me.
I stand in awe and wonder at the immensity of your
love.
I receive your grace and forgiveness. Open me to share
that with others.
Enable me to be merciful as I reach out to my hurting
brothers and sisters.
Visionary God, keep me clear and undistracted.
I admit there is much in my life that can clutter up
my relationship with you.
My desire is to be pure in heart. Loving Jesus, grant
me the blessing of your presence so that I may keep
my focus on you.
Prince of Peace, I lament the strife and struggles that

so mark human life. There are wars and terrorism, prejudice and hatred all over our world. Families are divided by harsh words and bitterness.

Lord, I confess that my own words and actions can be unloving.

Bless my desire to become a peacemaker, that this world may be a better place as together with all your people we do not tire of sowing peace.

Jesus who spoke truth and died because of it, give me courage to abide in you.

When there is hostility or opposition, may I not give in to timidity or fear but stand firm.

May I persevere in living for your kingdom of justice, mercy, and love, even if that brings danger or suffering.

God of glory, I receive your blessings. Help me continue to get the full life that you created in me, free to fully experience my humanity and to use that to bring blessings to everyone with whom I am in contact today.

In Jesus I pray, amen.

# ENDNOTES

1 John Bunyan, *The Pilgrim's Progress* (Harmandsworth, England: Penguin Books, 1965), p. 74.

2 Thich Nhat Hanh, in Erik Kolbell, *What Jesus Meant: The Beatitudes and a Meaningful Life* (Louisville: Westminster John Knox Press, 2003), p. 114.

3 Helmut Theilicke, *The Waiting Father: Sermons on the Parables of Jesus* (New York: Harper and Row, 1959), p.43.

4 Nicholas Wolterhoff, in James C. Howell, *The Beatitudes For Today* (Louisville: Westminster John Knox Press, 2006), p. 50.

5 Erik Kolbell, *op. cit.*, p. 43.

6 James C. Howell, *op. cit.*, p .41.

7 Erik Kolbell, *op. cit.,* p. 63.

8 Jim Forest, *The Ladder of the Beatitudes* (Maryknoll NY: Orbis Books, 1999), p. 60.

9 Erik Kolbell, *op. cit.,* p. 67-8.

10 James C. Howell, *op. cit.*, p. 53.

11 Giovanni Papini, in Erik Kolbell, *op. cit.*, p. 63.

12 From Robert A. Wallace, *Fire in the Bones* (Toronto: The United Church Publishing House, 1990), p. 47.

13 Lloyd Ogilve, *Congratulations, God Believes in You* (Waco: Word Books, 1980), p. 80.

14 James C. Howell, *op. cit.*, p. 66.

15 Brad Hambrick, *Vulnerability: Blessing in the Beatitudes* (Philadelphia: P&R Publishing, 2012), p. 22.

16 *Ibid,* p. 23.

17 Yevgeny Yevtushenko, in Jim Forest, *op. cit.*, p. 37.

18 Adapted from Marcus Borg, *The Heart of Christianity: Rediscovering a Life of Faith* (New York: HarperOne, 2003), p. 152-3.

19 Simon Tugwell, *The Beatitudes: Soundings in Christian Tradition* (Springfield Ill: Templegate Publishers, 1980), p. 94-5

20 Helen Keller, in David Legge, *The Beatitudes*, www.preachtheword.com

21 Simon Tugwell, *op. cit.*, p.103.

22 The full story of Sadako can be found in Eleanor Coerr, *Sadako and the Thousand Paper Cranes* (New York: G. P. Putnam's Sons, 1977).

23 From the *Report on Mission 7: Great Lakes Region, January – April 2012,* Blog on www.justequipping.org.

24 James C. Howell, *op. cit.*, p. 88.

25 Xu Yonghai, in Max Lucado, *Outlive Your Life* (Nashville: Thomas Nelson, 2010), p. 81.

26 G. K. Chesterton, in James C. Howell, *op. cit.*, p. 88.

27 Jim Forest, *op. cit.*, p. 156.

28 N. T. Wright, in Andy Crouch, *Culture Making: Recovering Our Creative Calling* (Downers Grove Ill: IVP Books, 2008), p. 261-2.

29 Tim Elmore, *Habitudes: Images That Form Leadership Habits and Attitudes* (Atlanta: Growing Leaders, Inc., 2004), p. 49.